Life after Grief:
How to Survive Loss and Trauma

Life after Grief

*How to Survive
Loss and Trauma*

Mel Lawrenz
and Daniel Green

Strategic Christian Living Series

Baker Books

A Division of Baker Book House Co
Grand Rapids, Michigan 49516

Published by Baker Books
a division of Baker Book House Company
P.O. Box 6287, Grand Rapids, MI 49516-6287

Printed in the United States of America

Library of Congress Cataloging-in-Publication Data

Lawrenz, Mel.
    Life after grief : how to survive loss and trauma / Mel Lawrenz and Daniel Green.
        p.   cm. —(Strategic Christian living)
    ISBN 0-8010-5268-8 (pbk.)
    1. Grief—Religious aspects—Christianity. 2. Bereavement—Religious aspects—Christianity. 3. Consolation. 4. Spiritual healing.
    I. Green, Daniel (Daniel R.)   II. Title. III. Series.
    BV4905.2L28   1995
    248.8'6—dc20   95-16828

to Mary Frances Haynes
in memorium

Contents

Acknowledgments

There are many people—teachers, coworkers, authors of books—who may be acknowledged as having taught us about grief and trauma.

But it is the participants themselves, the mourners, who deserve more credit than anyone. As a pastor and a psychologist we have many opportunities to meet people who suddenly come to a time of serious loss in life, and then have begun the journey of grieving. A great many of them express along the way the desire to be able to help other people going through loss in their lives. They have and they are. Their experience is part and parcel of this work. In particular, our friend Mary Haynes, in the three years in which she battled the cancer that eventually defeated her body at age 32, gave unselfishly (as did her husband, Don) in the interest of helping people face the reality of pain and loss, and also of God's grace and truth.

Our wives, Ingrid and Lynne, helped not only in their support but in their active, thoughtful involvement in the development of the central ideas of this book.

Final thanks to the editorial staff of Baker Books and to the staffs of Elmbrook Church and New Life Resources, Inc. with whom we have the privilege of working.

9

1

What Are Grief and Trauma?

"Blessed are those who mourn, for they will be comforted."
—Matthew 5:4

The Purpose of This Book

You are reading this book probably because you have come to a point of loss in your life or know someone else who has. And if not, you will.

It is one of life's certainties. We gain, and we lose. If we lose something or someone dear to us that loss can feel more painful than the tearing off of a limb. We may experience powerful tides of sadness, anger, frustration, hurt, fear, or shame. Our thinking may become clouded, we may be disoriented, sensing that we are incapable of making decisions. We may not trust ourselves.

If the crisis is prolonged we may deal with discouragement, resentment, or hopelessness. We may wonder how we will be able to go on.

This book is about grief and trauma. Grief and trauma are two different things, but they have in common the experience of losing someone or something. Both of them are well-charted waters that others have navigated—and gotten through—before us. Yet there is a great deal of confusion about how we get through loss. People who stand outside the experience of the mourner often do not understand, and then the mourner has to deal with that too.

Most important for us to understand is that there is hope. Even though death forces itself upon the human race relentlessly—real, physical death, but also the other "deaths" that characterize this world like abandonment, poverty, and disease—life still has a way of asserting itself. God has made us with powerful abilities to survive and regenerate. Finding his presence in the face of loss is what gives us hope.

There are many questions that mourners hold in common, questions that will be addressed chapter by chapter in this book:

- What's happening to me?
- Why is this happening?
- How long will this take?
- Why me?
- Where is God in all this?
- What can I do to help myself?

To try to answer these questions we will look both *up* and *out*: *up* to the spiritual resources that God provides for those wounded souls he loves so much; and *out* to the common experiences of those who have survived and recovered from loss. If there is comfort, it is to be found in knowing that we are not alone. There is a God who has said he will stand with us and for us; and there are others, many others, who have walked the same path, come to the same pitfalls and precipices, and have emerged.

What Is Grief?

Grief is the natural, expected reaction to a loss. Each word in that definition is important.

1. Grief is *natural.* In the normal course of life we all live through times of grief. It is not a sickness or a malady. It is not a sign that we are weak or inadequate; rather, it is a sign that some very good things have happened in our lives, for the only way to sense loss is if we really had something important.

It is not natural in the sense that we seek it, want it, or have to live constantly under its shadow, but rather in the sense that it is universal in human experience. The only way to avoid grief altogether is to live in a world where there is no loss. Now some Christians insist that in Christ they have all sufficiency, that loss is gain, and that Christians "do not grieve like the rest of men" (1 Thess. 4:13). The Bible does say all those things, but it does not thereby say that there is no such thing as loss and the grief resulting from loss. The Bible talks about grief and mourning from beginning to end and describes the mourning of some of its central characters: Jacob, Joseph, David, Jeremiah, Paul, and Jesus himself. The Bible holds forth the promise that God will heal us of grief, but not bypass it. Christians do not need "to grieve *like* the rest of men, *who have no hope*," but that doesn't mean they don't grieve at all.

2. Grief is *expected.* In other words, it is not abnormal to grieve in the face of loss. And when the loss is severe it is not abnormal to grieve powerfully or for a long time. It is not possible to be prepared for a major loss in one's life, nor should one think that one has to be strong enough in the present moment for any possible loss or tribulation. Oftentimes God's strength and grace comes only when the need arises. On the other hand, it is a great disadvantage to be naive about life, plunging ahead fully expecting that one will always get, and keep, what one wants. That may be the

case for a young person who has not had to face any significant loss, or who has always been given whatever he or she wants. Severe loss will always feel surprising or shocking, but we should not be surprised that this *kind* of thing happens in life.

Grief has purpose. It is a passageway, of sorts, from one form of life to another, a journey that must be traveled. When you lose someone in death, for instance, the painful process of grief allows you to adjust to a world that has been changed. One has to adjust when that father isn't there anymore to ask advise of, or the wife isn't there to nurture the kids, or the job has disappeared and it's necessary to seek training for a different profession.

3. Grief is a *reaction*. It is dynamic; it is often powerful. It may begin with the internal reaction of the heart, but then follow consequences in our relationships, in our life's functions, and even in our bodies.

A teenage boy's mother dies unexpectedly. He is at first stunned, then furious, then depressed. He withdraws from his siblings and friends, and then, to medicate his pain, begins drinking excessively, which only worsens his depression. Before long he is not sleeping or eating properly and has all but dropped out of school. There is not an area of his life that is not reacting to the awful severing of losing his mother.

It is because of the potential power of grief that we need people outside us to help us get a sense of perspective, and to judge what kind of help we need.

A grief reaction may be much less severe under other circumstances. The young mother whose first child leaves for the first time on the school bus may very well have a stabbing sense of loss. Her baby is growing up, there is no way of stopping it. It is not that she is not glad for the maturing of her little boy. But something she had before is different now. The sense of grief that first week of school will help her adapt to a new stage of life.

4. Finally, grief is the result of *loss*. There are the obvious losses we're all familiar with: a loved one dies, or moves away, or contracts a serious disease. Almost any kind of life issue can result in loss. You can lose money, lose your home, lose status, lose security, lose credibility. The loss may be physical, it may be relational, or it may simply be psychological. If there is a perception of loss there will be grief. Whether the experience is simple sadness or outright mourning there is a message to listen to, a lesson to learn.

A Word about Mourning

Mourning is the outward expression of grief. It is what people on the outside see: for example, the mourner's crying or withdrawal or fits of emotion. It can take the form of ritual (although much less today than in the past), the best example being the funeral. These outward expressions of grief are extremely important in the healing process. They

help the mourner release the energy of emotion;
communicate to others what the loss means to the mourner;
help affirm the value of what or who was lost;
publicly validate that the mourner's reactions are legitimate.

This last point is so important, because when we lose someone or something valuable to us part of our healing consists in acknowledging and recollecting the value of what was lost. There is no comfort in devaluing what was lost; we want to and should be able to carry with us into the future a full (and realistic) sense of the worth of what we lost. If other people suggest otherwise they are only adding loss on top of loss. For example, how often those who have stillborn children hear something like "at least you didn't really get to know the child," or "it's a good thing you didn't take him home," or "you can have other children."

Mourning is for mourners. While certain rites like funerals may be a way of showing respect for the deceased, the grief process itself does not benefit the deceased. Mourners should release any such ideas so that *they* can move through the process of grief that will ultimately help them to come to grips with and adjust to the loss.

What Is Trauma?

Most of this book will deal with the normal forms of grief that result from normal losses. There are many people, however, whose loss comes with such severity that it is best described as *trauma*. Chapters 8 and 9 of this book deal with the special circumstances of traumatic loss.

Trauma is the experience of something shocking happening to someone (physically or psychologically) that produces some kind of inner injury and affects the person's ability to function in normal ways. There are three parts to this definition: shock, injury, and function.

1. The external *shock* is an event that is significantly influential; something that shakes a person's assumptions or sense of well-being. It truly affects a person at the moment and for a long time afterwards. The most common experiences resulting in trauma would be things like a severe auto accident, death of someone very close, rape or other forms of sexual abuse, being the victim of a crime, or witnessing such events. Sometimes it is the unexpectedness that makes trauma so jarring. Trauma visits in its unexpected way when a person who thought he'd get to work like any normal day instead ends up in intensive care because of an auto accident, or the person who gets a call at work that his or her house is in flames, or the person who is held up at gunpoint just a block from home. Trauma is not always the result of

a surprising event. The rapid progress of cancer can lead someone into several jarring stages of trauma. Each visit to the doctor and progressively worse blood count is a blow to the morale and security of the patient and his or her loved ones.

2. Trauma results in *injury*, a wounding of the inner life. There is no uniform list of traumatic events because different people are susceptible to inner injury to different degrees. Death of a loved one may be traumatic, but not necessarily so. If your father dies in his later years you may go through a fairly normal grief reaction in the months after the funeral, but if you had an extraspecial closeness, or dependency, the loss may throw you into depression and other complicated forms of mourning. Your inner life has not just been jolted, but deeply injured.

3. An inability to *function* properly is the consequence of real trauma. Physical difficulties, depression, withdrawal from relationships, irrational fears, emotional swings or emotional repression are some of the many evidences that a traumatic event or events have had damaging effects. A person may feel like he or she repeatedly relives the incident. Christians are not immune to such experiences any more than they are immune to physical disease. They have tremendous spiritual resources available to them, but they are still affected by the shocking events of trauma.

In the long run, it is possible to become a survivor rather than a victim, as was the case of the apostle Paul who was severely mistreated but who could say: "We are hard pressed on every side, but not crushed; perplexed, but not in despair; persecuted, but not abandoned; struck down, but not destroyed" (2 Cor. 4:8–9).

Myths about Grief

Throughout this book we will encounter and address the most common myths about grief—myths that stand in the

way of the necessary process of grieving, and that sometimes result in very unhelpful reactions from those on the
outside. When you grieve, unfortunately you have to expect
that you will hear some things from others who mean well,
but who really don't understand grief. These myths include
the following:

- grief (or prolonged grief) is a sign of lack of faith
- only weak people grieve
- all mourners need to do to resolve their grief is to get
  their feelings out
- to get past grief what you need to do is get the loss out
  of your mind
- mourning should not last more than three months and
  certainly not more than a year
- grief tapers off evenly and predictably with the passage of time
- the way you mourn is the measure of how much you
  loved the one you lost
- each loss is grieved separately

Entering the House of Mourning

Don't ever let someone tell you there is something wrong
with you if you are grieving. You are walking through a valley, and the shadows can look foreboding and cold. Yet, if
you keep walking, you will emerge. Or, to use an analogy
from the Old Testament:

> It is better to go to a house of mourning than to go to a house
> of feasting, for death is the destiny of every man; the living
> should take this to heart. Sorrow is better than laughter, be-
> cause a sad face is good for the heart. The heart of the wise
> is in the house of mourning, but the heart of fools is in the
> house of pleasure (Eccles. 7:2–4).

A "sad face is good for the heart," not all the time, but when it is the only honest response to a genuine loss. To paste on a false smile may make others more comfortable (and that's why they don't want you to grieve), but it may only prolong your grief.

God doesn't ask us to take up permanent residence in the house of mourning, but when we do mourn we need to visit that house, learn what must be learned there, and come out stronger for it. When Jesus said "Blessed are those who mourn, for they will be comforted," he was telling us that because loss is inevitable in the kind of world we live in, so is mourning; but so also is the promise of God's restoration.

2

What's Happening to Me?— The Experience of Loss

"Be merciful to me, O LORD, for I am in distress; my eyes grow weak with sorrow, my soul and my body with grief. My life is consumed by anguish and my years by groaning; my strength fails because of my affliction, and my bones grow weak."

—Psalm 31:9–10

The house of mourning is not a comfortable place. It hurts, confuses, and scares us. Not knowing what is happening or if what we are feeling is normal can be frightening and depressing. On the other hand, having an understanding of what is happening can help ease fears and help us make sense out of what we are experiencing.

Each person mourns in a unique way, in a manner that is shaped by his or her unique characteristics and previous life experiences. How we express grief will differ from one person to another, and it will change for us as we proceed through the grief process. Normal grieving takes many

21

forms. As there is no one "right" way to mourn, not everyone will experience all of the responses that are described
in this chapter. Furthermore, we experience these reactions
in varying intensities and at different times. The following
descriptions of the grief experience are offered as examples of the experience of mourning and illustrate that grieving involves the whole person.

Emotional Reactions

"I was asked today if I still have a hole in my heart—I feel
like I have the Grand Canyon." This observation came from
a woman who had many months earlier experienced the
death of her husband. Significant losses produce strong
emotion in us, reactions which can ultimately be very helpful but are often experienced as painful.

We have been created with a wonderful warning system
which not only alerts us to changes but also influences our
energy levels to help us cope. Our emotions are physical
reactions to our perception of changes. These changes may
be something outside of us or something internal, such as
a hope or expectation.

We may think of our emotional reactions as a kind of internal weather. At times, the air is calm and stable with the
sun warming us and a gentle breeze moving past us. At other
times the air currents change, bringing storms and turbu-
lence. The rain that is needed for life may come gently or
at times violently; the rain may come when needed or at in-
convenient times. We always experience weather, although
we may not always be aware of it. Often it is only the beau-
tiful or the extreme weather that captures our attention.

In a similar manner, we are continually experiencing
emotional reactions. At times we feel them and are aware
of them, while at other times our emotions are affecting us
without our awareness. By becoming aware of what we are

feeling we can benefit from the information emotions provide and make choices about resolving them.

Can the painful emotions of grief ever be helpful? Why does it hurt so much? Will I be able to get through this? These and other questions point to the pain of grief, a pain which can be magnified if we are unaware of the purpose of these reactions.

Emotions are reactions, and, as such, are the result of encountering other things; for instance, the behavior of others (external) or our own memories (internal). We can learn to identify the object of the emotional reaction (what we are reacting to), which can help in choosing how to respond. Emotions also provide information to us about the object and about what is changing in our lives. In this way, emotional reactions function like signals and help us to adjust to our changing surroundings.

Table 2.1 provides an overview of our basic emotional reactions and the information they provide. When you become aware of an emotional reaction you can ask yourself "what am I feeling" and "what am I reacting to?" At times we can begin by identifying our feelings which in turn direct us to the message of the emotions. At other times the reverse is true: we are aware of the message and can then determine what we are feeling.

Grief and trauma involve the experience of loss which in turn activates the emotion of sadness. The initial news or realization that a loss has occurred often produces a sense of shock. The surprise of the loss, even in situations in which the loss was anticipated, can stun and paralyze a person. At this point the individual may feel numb or overwhelmed. Like a tidal wave that engulfs a small island, the emotions may sweep over the person leaving him or her with a drowning sensation.

As the reality of the loss begins to sink in, we are likely to feel great pain. We cry out that something is wrong, very wrong, and we are angry. "The death shouldn't have hap-

Table 2.1

Emotions and Their Functions

Emotion	Purpose, Information Provided
joy, happiness	continue, this is good
acceptance	affiliation, safety
anticipation	this is new, explore
surprise	unexpected, stop and get oriented, be alert
disgust	reject, this is "poison," push away
anger	something is wrong or I have been wronged; change something in my situation or within myself to correct the wrong
sadness	a loss has occurred; adjust to the loss, adapt to being without what was lost; accept; let go of control
fear	danger is present; I must change the situation, learn to cope within the situation, or escape/avoid the situation; fight, flight, or cope
hurt	I have been harmed or abused; discontinue or avoid
shame	I want to hide; I feel disconnected from someone, I want to reconnect

pened!" and "I want him (or her) back!" For many the anger swells up inside with no apparent specific cause. "I'm just so angry—I don't know who to be angry at" was how one woman put it in reference to the death of her husband. At times we may be aware that we are angry, while at other times we sense tension and are aware that things are not right, not the way we believe they should be.

Fear often sets in when we acknowledge that things are not as they should be. Fear of the unknown, fear of how I'll live without the deceased, fear of how I'll make it on my own. Fear signals that we may be facing a dangerous situation or one that we interpret as dangerous. We may be afraid of our anger, or angry at our fear. Do I have a right to be angry? Is it okay to be angry with someone who died?

Many people become afraid of the pain of grief. Mourners often say, "I didn't know I could hurt this much," and may describe times when the pain engulfed them as if they were helpless in the pain, as if a part of them was being ripped out. Attempts to avoid the pain often only intensify it, and the delay in experiencing the pain is offset by the depth of the pain later felt.

Fear suggests that we may be facing danger since dangerous situations often involve pain. However, as much as the pain of grief hurts, *this kind of pain is not harmful.* Our hurting is not harmful or dangerous; rather, our hurting is necessary for us to adjust to the loss we have encountered. This pain, even though it may seem unrelenting, will help us let go of what we do not have so that we can live realistically in the present.

We may feel shame upon the death of a loved one as we become painfully aware of our vulnerability and our disconnection from him or her. Shame is felt when we notice we are disconnected from someone else or from our own expectations and values. Death is an irreversible disconnection in human relationships. We may feel like hiding or have thoughts of guilt. Often survivors ask themselves, "What could I have done?" or say, "If only I had . . ." as a way of trying to resolve the pain of their shame reaction. How can I reconnect with someone removed by death?

Mary Beth was shocked that her husband of ten years was now dead. Who could she be angry with? Night was the worst. Putting the children to bed and then facing the quiet house and the empty bedroom scared her. She was afraid to clean out his closet and drawers—maybe this would end her last connection with him. Yet the constant reminders of him when she ran across his personal articles brought forth great pain, anger, fear, and sadness. One evening she "lost it." Taking her child's whiffleball bat, she began hitting her bed and crying out as loudly as she could. At first, the pain intensified. In her anger she dumped his drawers on the floor, crying out "why did you leave me?" Mary Beth yelled, cried, sobbed, and hit her bed as she tried to let go of the emotional pain she felt. Exhausted, she slept on top of her covers that night.

The next morning Mary Beth looked around her, saw her husband's clothing and other personal items around the room, and cried some more. She gathered some boxes and began to sort it all out. Some she kept out, some she put away for storage, and others she chose to give away. Her anger had allowed her to break the grip her fear had on her, allowing her to take the next step in adjusting to her loss. Her pain motivated her to make a change, to continue to adjust to what she had lost. On the other side of her pain she began to find peace.

Sadness is resolved when we adjust to what we have lost. Sadness slows us down so that we focus on the loss and adjust our expectations, routines, habits, and hopes. As we make these adjustments the sadness decreases. In a similar manner, anger is resolved when we respond to the wrong, or the object of the anger. At the time of a death, we may be angry that the deceased is not with us, that we will not realize our dreams and hopes together. Our anger is resolved as we let go of these expectations and hopes, as we accept the way things are and release our demand for how we want them to be. We can resolve our shame as we connect with what is real, accepting both what has been lost and what remains. At times of grief this emotional reaction can prompt us to face our disconnection, our loss. Mourning changes us. As grief is resolved, the emotional reactions of happiness, anticipation, and joy return. Initially mourners may not notice they are feeling well and may even be surprised if someone points this out. They may feel ashamed at feeling happy, as if their happiness may separate them from the deceased or look as if they don't care. Many who have deeply mourned say that they were able eventually to come to feel a deeper joy than they had before their loss, that experiencing the depths of pain had introduced them to vistas of other emotions they had not previously known. Yet a sense of the loss, a shadow of the sadness, may be present even in these joyful times.

Physical Reactions

The experience of severe loss even affects our bodies. Upon initially hearing the news of the loss, we may feel a choking or suffocating sensation and feel dizzy or faint. We may sense exhaustion, lack of physical strength, paralysis, trembling, shaking, twitching, heart palpitations, and nausea, diarrhea, or other gastrointestinal distress. Shortness of breath or rapid, shallow breathing may occur and swallowing may be difficult. Some people describe feeling as if something is stuck in their throat. Headaches or other body pains may occur. The body is likely to be tense with involuntary muscle spasms occurring in some situations. Chest pains, hot flashes or chills, excessive sweating, and a dry mouth may also be experienced. These physical symptoms may last just a few minutes or much longer, even reoccurring weeks and months later.

Sleeping and eating are often disrupted. For some, sleep is an escape through which they can get away from the pain; they sleep excessively as a way of avoiding waking life. For others, sleep is difficult. One woman said that she hated

going to sleep because each time she woke up she again encountered the reality and pain that she was alone in her
bed, that her husband was really dead. Others have nightmares or dreams involving the person or object they lost.
They may wake during the night and, depending on whether
the dream was pleasant or painful, may want to return to
the dream or avoid sleep altogether. In a similar manner,
eating may be affected. Some eat excessively for comfort
while others lose their appetites.

These physical symptoms of grief tend to decrease with
time but may reoccur suddenly and unexpectedly at such
times as an anniversary of the loss, holidays, or the deceased person's birthday. "Just when I thought I was doing
okay I started to feel that choking and suffocating feeling"
is how one widow put it. At first she was fearful that she
was going to reexperience all the pain of her initial grief,
and was relieved when these symptoms subsided after a
few hours. Some people experience a return of these physical symptoms years after the loss.

Thoughts, Beliefs, and Expectations

Grieving interferes with our ability to concentrate, focus
our attention, think, solve problems, and remember even
simple things. Simple problems seem overwhelming. "I
can't even follow the directions on a cake box" commented
a woman whose child had recently died. "I can't remember where I put anything, I forgot which child went to
which school, and sometimes I'll just stand in the store in
a daze, not sure where I am or what I'm supposed to be
doing."

The initial reaction is often disbelief. "This can't be real"
is often the feeling during the first days, weeks, and even
months. Many mourning rituals, such as a funeral or an
open casket—difficult as they are—help mourners accept
the reality of the loss.

A preoccupation with the loss, continued and persistent thoughts of the loss (ruminations), and the avoidance of any reminders of the loss may occur. A phone ringing, footsteps in the next room, or a car pulling into the driveway may all cue the expectation that the deceased person is still around, that he or she is home once again.

People have an inherent need to make sense out of what is happening to them, to understand their lives. Beliefs about ourselves can be changed as our vulnerability and inadequacy are exposed through the loss. Mourning people often are pessimistic and highly critical of themselves and others. They are more likely to blame themselves for negative events and may experience disillusionment and a loss of purpose or hope. Some will blame themselves for the loss or death, no matter how illogical this conclusion may be.

Mourners often ask "why?" "why me?" "why them?" "why now?" One's existing beliefs may be inadequate to account for what happened, to make sense out of the loss and pain. Where is God in this? Why did God allow this?

Many mourners wish our culture still had visible signs and rituals indicating that a person was mourning. Some decades back it was common for a widow to wear black for a full year after the death of her spouse. To some today that notion appears morose, but there was one woman who said she wished the custom still prevailed. Two weeks after the death of her husband she brought her son's bicycle into a bike shop for a flat tire to be fixed. When the store owner said (in a way that he thought was being helpful), "Doing this isn't so hard. You should have your old man do it," the widow was stunned. She knew she couldn't resent what the man had said, after all, how could he know? Yet his very ignorance hurt. Looking back on the incident much later she remarked, "I wish widows still wore black."

Some mourners have difficulty again having fun or pleasure in their lives as they do not want to communicate that everything is fine. Others are afraid that it is inappropriate to enjoy life after such a loss. Such uncertainty leaves many feeling very alone.

Values change as a result of mourning. A man who experienced the death of his young son commented, "Work no longer seems so important. I look forward to getting home and being with my family." It has been said that no one ever said on his death bed, "I wish I had worked more." Grieving is a lens that may bring into focus what is most important to us; it clarifies what we truly value. We feel the pain because what we have lost was treasured by us. Following the loss we can attend to those things of value in our lives.

Perceptions

The basic building blocks of experience are perceptions; i.e., the mental processes by which we recognize and interpret our experiences. These elemental aspects of our experience can be altered during grief such that a mourner may be uncertain about what is real. Following the death of a loved one, it is common for mourners to sense that they heard the deceased or saw them in a familiar place. Others sense their presence with them at a specific time. The deceased may be experienced as silent or as having a message, such as that they are fine in heaven. Such experiences are described as startling yet comforting. For others, such experiences are scary. Mourners often are reluctant to share such experiences with others, fearing that others will not understand and may even think they are "going crazy."

Feelings of unreality, or as if a person is separated from himself or herself, may also occur during mourning. While attending the funeral of his father, and for several days afterward, a young man described himself as a robot going through the motions while he seemed removed and a spectator. He said he felt nothing, as if he did all the things expected of him on automatic pilot. Later he could barely remember those events.

Attempts at Coping

"This can't be, no, no, no!" sobbed a young woman, mother of two children, after being informed that her husband had been killed in a car accident. Several months later, she continued to live as if he were soon to come home from a business trip. Yes, she acknowledged that he was gone, that he had died and his body was buried, yet she was aware she did not want to let go of the hope he would again pull up in the driveway and walk into the kitchen.

All of us develop coping strategies for living in a sinful world. We can often protect ourselves from painful realities with what psychologists call defense mechanisms. These mechanisms often function in a healthy manner, protecting us from thoughts and feelings that may overwhelm us and interfere with our ability to live and function in the present.

Many of us initially respond to loss with denial. This response may be an actual refusal to believe or act in a manner appropriate to the loss that has occurred. Denial can also be manifested through emotional numbing and disbelief, even in the face of clear evidence of the loss.

Others may repress or suppress any thoughts or feelings about the loss, removing them from their awareness. They may acknowledge the loss and may even give themselves a brief time to mourn publicly, but then not allow feelings or thoughts involving the loss. Some find themselves regressing to an earlier stage of life, possibly feeling very dependent and helpless. Mourners may experience a strong identification with the deceased, assuming the characteristics, interests, and even mannerisms of the loved one. In doing so, they may sense some temporary connection.

For many, the use of such defensive strategies are short-lived and allow the person to begin the adjustment process. Sometimes these defensive strategies become inadequate or too rigid and the coping strategy may actually interfere with their ability to function well. The inflexible coping style may prohibit the changes that mourning demands. At such times the mourner may benefit from counseling or psychotherapy.

Activities and Social Relationships

Grief disrupts daily activities, even such basic activities as eating and sleeping. Any activity which involved the loss will likely seem disorganized, as if a piece is missing. John, an elderly widower, discovered after many weeks that he no longer drank coffee with his morning paper since his wife had died. She had always made the coffee and he had associated the event of breakfast and reading the paper with her. He continued to do what he had always done; her parts were initially left undone. This sense of having a part of your life missing contributes to the confusion, disorganization, and absentmindedness experienced by many mourners.

Often mourners find themselves scanning their surroundings looking for their loved ones. Others avoid activities which had involved the deceased. Meal time may be especially difficult as there is an empty space, a place where the loved person "should be." Attending church, going to dinner, or even to a friend's house alone can be very lonely and painful.

Social relationships are forever impacted by a significant loss. For many, a loss impacts their ability to be vulnerable. Some feel overly exposed and helpless while others retreat from people in an attempt to feel safe. Some mourners lose interest in other people while others desire constant companionship and may fear being alone. In both situations, mourners are likely to focus on their experience, unable to respond well to others.

Feelings of envy or jealousy may occur when the mourner is around those who have not had a similar loss.

Such feelings may then evoke feelings of shame and thoughts of guilt. Many sense that only those who have had a similar loss can really understand their experience or accept them. To cope with the distress, some engage in self-destructive or risk-taking behaviors. Some mourners begin to abuse alcohol and other substances, including prescription tranquilizers. Mourners tend to be accident prone. Others act impulsively or act out, possibly as a means of sedating or blunting their pain.

Grief will bring changes to a mourner's life. With time and many adjustments new patterns and habits develop. New relationships are developed while existing relationships grow and change. Some relationships may be lost in the adjustment process. When we leave the house of mourning, we are different.

The effects of loss, any type of loss, are significant. Every part of our existence—our mind, soul, heart, body, and relationships—are affected. Some of these changes may persist throughout our lives. Naturally, we tend to seek relief, and often we do so by trying to make sense out of what has happened.

3

Why Is This Happening?—
The Problem of Suffering

"Why must I go about mourning, oppressed by the enemy?"
—Psalm 42:9

The Big Question—Why?

When we are plunged into grief, our minds may fixate on one simple question: "Why?" For some it is an occasional wondering, for others a relentless searching. It is rooted in our desire to find meaning in life and our not wanting to feel like we are random victims of chance—or worse, some wicked power. We wonder why it couldn't be the other way, why we couldn't have held onto what we lost. Did I not deserve what I had? Did I make some mistake? Am I being punished? Is God not able to protect what is good? It is regrettable when such questions stand as a barrier between a mourner and God, for it is in times of grief that we need God the most.

These are not easy questions, and some people, conse-
quently, try to pretend that they never come up—at least
not in the minds of faithful people.

Yet for some reason God saw fit to include in the Bible
many instances when those who believed in him came to
those questions when they faced loss. If we have such questions we might as well be honest about them. Instead of
being a sign of a lack of faith, they can be the active searching of faith that wants to grow.

The Psalms, which give us such a vivid picture of how
our hearts work, include numerous instances when God's
faithful asked these tough questions. David, who experienced loss in many forms (persecution, death, betrayal, rejection) put it this way in Psalm 10:

> Why, O Lord, do you stand far off? Why do you hide your-
> selves in times of trouble . . . ? Arise, Lord! Lift up your hand,
> O God. Do not forget the helpless. Why does the wicked
> man revile God? Why does he say to himself, "He won't call
> me to account"? But you, O God, do see trouble and grief;
> you consider it to take it in hand. The victim commits him-
> self to you; you are the helper of the fatherless. . . . You hear,
> O Lord, the desire of the afflicted; you encourage them, and
> you listen to their cry, defending the fatherless and the op-
> pressed.

God Knows

Even though David asked why it seemed that God was
absent from his circumstances, in his heart he knew better.
He had a lot of why questions, but he knew that God knew.
"You, O God, do see trouble and grief, you consider it to
take it in hand. . . . You hear, O Lord, the desire of the af-
flicted . . . you listen to their cry."

God knows. He is not ignorant of our losses, nor is he in-
different about them. The fact that losses occur does not

mean that God is absent or weak. God was there when the first humans experienced the first loss (a result of their own actions); and God will be there at the end of time to reconcile and restore much of what was lost.

Some people are frustrated that they don't get a very satisfying answer to the "why" question. They have asked friends or their pastors; they've read books, read the Bible. It's not that there are no answers available, but that an answer is not what is missing. What is really missing, what is really causing the pain, is what or who was lost. Even if you could get a completely satisfying answer to "why?" you would still sense the absence of that loved one who died or whatever the loss may be.

It's Not Just You and God

If grief or trauma produce a spiritual crisis, especially one where we doubt the love or the power or the goodness of God, it may be because we are missing some important pieces to the puzzle of life.

While God can and does act in direct ways in our lives, it would be a mistake to picture your world as just you and God, every action, good or bad, the direct effect of a God who acts like a puppet master, pulling the strings of your life in some uncertain and even dangerous dance. If that were the case we would be justified in asking: why did God put that malignant lump in my wife's breast? why did he cause the drunk driver to swerve over into my lane? why did he want that neighbor to abuse his children? why did he cause that boy to get a blood transfusion contaminated with the HIV virus? But those questions ignore many other factors.

No, it isn't just God and you. The Bible teaches clearly that we belong to a whole system known as humanity, and live in a world—the entire created world—that is at the present time given to corruption and decay. We live in a world that God "has given over" to its natural inclinations (Rom. 1:24ff.), or, to put it another way, a world "in bondage to corruption" and "frustrated." But God has ways of restoring us in the aftermath of loss in this world, and offers us an ultimate, final restoration in heaven.

You're Not the Only One Who Is Frustrated

Romans 8 has some of the most comforting words of the entire Bible ("we know that in all things God works for the good of those who love him"; "if God is for us, who can be against us?"; "who shall separate us from the love of Christ?"), but it also gives us an honest picture of a world in which loss has become a normal experience:

> The creation waits in eager expectation for the sons of God to be revealed. For the creation was *subjected to frustration,* not by its own choice, but by the will of the one who subjected it, in hope that the creation itself will be liberated from its *bondage to decay* and brought into the glorious freedom of the children of God. We know that the whole creation has been *groaning as in the pains of childbirth* right up to the present time. Not only so, but we ourselves, who have the firstfruits of the Spirit, *groan inwardly* as we *wait eagerly* for our adoption as sons, the *redemption* of our bodies. For in this *hope* we were saved (Rom. 8:19–24) [italics added].

There are three ideas repeated in this passage: a) the reality of suffering, b) the way suffering is experienced, and c) hope that extends beyond suffering.

While this passage speaks of the whole of creation, is it not a picture of any person experiencing grief? What Paul here calls "frustration" and "groaning" may translate in our experience into sadness, crying, depression, fear, anger, or rage. Loss comes as an insult or an external assault. It hurts, it injures. It is an "inward groaning" because the frustration

THE REALITY OF LOSS	THE EXPERIENCE OF FRUSTRATION	THE HOPE FOR SOMETHING BETTER
"present sufferings"	"subjected to frustration"	"eager expectation"
"bondage to decay"	"groaning"	"in hope"
"pains of childbirth"	"groan inwardly"	"we wait eagerly"

occurs at the center of our inner lives. Grief is indeed a kind of spiritual crisis. Beyond emotion and beyond intellectual questioning, it is the sense of disjunction or displacement in our souls—the sense that "this is not the way things are supposed to be." It's not just you, it's the condition of the whole world.

In All Things God Works

There is still the question of purpose. We want to believe that if we suffer loss it will not be empty and purposeless. And so we ask "why?" But we must be careful here. It is hard to find a purpose behind a child being raped or a wife being berated and demeaned by her husband or a village being leveled by an earthquake. The Bible depicts such things as the painful events of a creation in bondage to frustration. If we force ourselves to find a specific divine purpose in such events we only end up creating confusion about God, about morality, and about the world we live in.

Yet this does not mean we are cast adrift in a disturbed and violent world. God is still Lord of the universe, the only one who knows past, present, and future; the only one who can take the graces and blessings of life, work them together with the losses we experience, and keep us whole. God is working all the time; he is at work when we gain a blessing; and he works at times when we have lost someone or something dear to us.

It is not surprising that Christians quote Romans 8:28 as often as they do:

> And we know that in all things God works for the good of those who love him, who have been called according to his purpose.

It speaks of purpose and of a connection with God; it tells us something about the tapestry of the events of our lives—that is, that God continues to work "in all things."

Unfortunately, the meaning of this verse has often been twisted into the following shape: God is good, God works all things together for the good, therefore everything that happens must be good and you should try to discover God's intent in bringing about the losses you experience.

But that is not what the verse says. Rather, it says that God (because he is good) works toward the good and that he is doing so at all times under all circumstances ("in all things") and his goodness will ultimately prevail. Murder is not a good thing, neither is cancer, adultery, starvation, and impoverishment, enmity, or unemployment. The grieving person does not have to translate a woeful loss into something good. Yet he or she can be assured that a sovereign God takes all circumstances under the sun, losses as well as gains, and is able to continue to work goodness into the lives of those he loves.

Landmarks of a Greater Purpose

There are many people who can and do testify to good things that have been built out of the rubble of their losses.

- A young mother dying of cancer who said that she learned more about love and priorities and the value of relationships than she had ever imagined possible.

- Many of her friends and family whose attitude toward their own lives took on a greater seriousness and reverence.

- A family who lost their house in a fire and learned about the things that endure—matters of the soul—and how their sense of family values was deepened and enlarged.

- A convicted criminal who went on to have a major ministry within the prisons and became an advocate of prison reform.

- A man who lost his father early, had to mature quickly, and was able to be effective in leadership as an adult.

- A couple who both came from terribly confused and conflictual families who nevertheless were able to be good and loving parents.

- A medic in Vietnam who saw great carnage, and who went on to become a pastor with a heart for the spiritual needs of people.

- A mother who lost her child in a drunk driving accident and who in the years that followed rallied many other similar mourners to affect the law of the land . . .

and many more.

One thing is indisputable: loss changes us. It will stress our weak points and strengthen our strengths. We are changed.

If you are presently in the darkest shadow of grief it may be hard to accept these words, hard to believe them, even hard to hear them. If that is the case, this may not be the time to try to figure it all out. Mourners will tell you that it took some time for them to perceive and appreciate the good that came out of their suffering. Changes like the development of a compassionate heart or a new value system don't happen overnight.

When the apostle Paul said "we know that suffering produces perseverance; perseverance, character; and character, hope," (Rom. 5:3–4) it was not theological theory, but out of his own experience of being beaten, imprisoned, rejected, and defamed. He also spoke of

> the Father of compassion and the God of all comfort, who comforts us in all our troubles, so that we can comfort those in any trouble with the comfort we ourselves have received from God (2 Cor. 1:3–4).

One of the most likely effects on our character is a greater ability to be compassionate and empathetic. Is there any doubt that the world could use more people with compassion and understanding in their hearts? Could anything be more important than what Jesus called "a new command": "Love one another. As I have loved you, so you must love one another" (John 13:34)?

Which brings us back to the purpose of grieving: an adjustment and rearrangement of our lives in the aftermath of loss. If you don't go through grieving, if the pain of loss stays locked and trapped inside, it may turn you bitter instead of better. If, on the other hand, you grieve and mourn in natural ways, there is a good chance you will come out with a larger heart, with something more to offer those around you, and with a greater appreciation of what is good. And that is part of what turns loss into gain.

4

How Long Will This Take?—
The Journey of Grieving

"How long, O LORD? Will you forget me forever? How long
will you hide your face from me? How long must I wrestle
with my thoughts and every day have sorrow in my heart?
How long will my enemy triumph over me?"

—Psalm 13:1–2

How long will this take, how long will I feel this way?
Will I grieve forever? What is going to happen to me? What's
next for me? All of life is disturbed; nothing seems the
same—will I ever get over this? These and similar questions
often come to mind during the grief process. We may find
comfort and a lessening of our fears by gaining an understanding of what is happening and a way of predicting what
may happen in the future.

In order to understand mourning it is important to understand the purpose of grief. We grieve so that we can adjust to loss, to the changes that have occurred in our lives.
Our grief cries out that something is very different, alarm-

ing us to the change and demanding that we adjust. The pain of grief motivates us to seek relief. Sorrow prompts adjustments in our thinking, feeling, expectations, beliefs, and activities. As these changes occur, the pain diminishes, the anguish lessens, and a new life can develop. Such changes are not easy. The work of grief is hard. Merely thinking about the loss does not give us relief from grief. Grieving involves our whole being, not just our thinking or feeling. Our understanding of mourning must include all of what makes us human—our mind, emotions, soul, and relationships.

The Grief Journey

Someone has said: "grief is not an address, but a process." People proceed through mourning by passing through stages or phases. We adjust to the news and then the reality of the loss incrementally. Grief is a journey which moves across mountains and valleys, foreboding deserts and lush oases. These different phases, or parts of the journey, can be accomplished only by moving through them. The journey progresses one step at a time. The progress made on the journey may seem slow, yet each step moves closer to the destination. Often progress can only be noticed after some time has elapsed and the traveler notices where he or she is and can look back at where he or she had been.

Each of us proceeds on our grief journey in a unique manner. Our personal history and current life situations shape our mourning, as does the nature of the loss, our relationship to the deceased, and the role the loss played in our lives. Our grief maps have common characteristics but are also uniquely formed. Furthermore, we progress on this trek in different and sometimes mysterious ways. Rather than following a straight path from point A to point B, we proceed step by step, sometimes moving ahead and at other times seemingly returning to a place of mourning we have previously visited. Mourners are often heard to say: "I thought I was over this."

The journey may progress differently for different aspects of our lives. For example, a widow may notice that she is far along the path of healing with regard to the role of spouse yet in a very different place as regards her role as parent. She may experience much difficulty in adjusting to being a single parent and find that she misses her husband most as an absent father.

The progression in grief is more like traveling in an upward spiral than in a straight line. Imagine a white candy cane with a red stripe. It has a front side and a back side. In order to follow the red line from the bottom to the top you will have to move from the front to the back and then again to the front of the cane. As you progress upwards you will alternate between the front and back.

Healing is similar to this upward progression. At times we may sense that we are doing very well (the front side) and then later we struggle (the back side). Alternating between these two may seem like we are not progressing, but in reality we are on the same side yet in a different place. Our healing journey will wind around and around as we progress.

Three Phases of Grief

Many psychological researchers and theorists have systematically studied the process of grief. We are helped greatly by understanding such road maps of the journey of grief. Several descriptions of the grief process have been developed which describe what happens when we are faced with a great loss. These models also identify the tasks or the work that needs to be accomplished and the process which we must proceed through in order to resolve our grief. Theories of grief serve as a map, helping mourners to identify where they are, see where they have come from, and understand where they are going.

The research and writings of Therese Rando have been found by many to be very helpful in describing this journey. She describes three phases of grief and six processes that a mourner proceeds through for grief resolution, for the arrival at the destination (see Table 4.1).

Avoidance Phase

The avoidance phase begins upon becoming aware of the death or other loss. The mind and body may go into a state of shock, a numbness in which everything may seem unreal. Overwhelmed, the mourner may be confused and unable to comprehend what is happening. He or she may become passive, even nonresponsive. Everything may seem disturbed, nothing may make sense, nothing may seem real.

As the initial shock diminishes and the reality of the loss begins to sink in, denial is likely. Statements like "this can't be" and "this isn't real" are often expressed. This denial of the reality of the death, of the recognition of the loss, is actually beneficial. The denial allows us time to absorb the reality of the news, to comprehend the gravity of what has happened. It allows us to take small steps, albeit often unsteady steps, in the beginning of the grief journey.

The denial reactions may alternate with intense emotional expressions of anger, sadness, fear, and protest. Many questions come rushing in, like "how did this happen?" or "why did this happen?"

The central process of the avoidance phase is to recognize the loss. The reality of a death is difficult to acknowledge or grasp. A mourner needs some confirmation of the death. Viewing the body and a funeral service are rituals that help in this acknowledgment.

The absence of such evidence of the reality of the death can delay and interfere with the grief process. One couple had concluded that their son had drowned in a sailing accident, although the body was not recovered. They were re-

Table 4.1

The Phases of Grieving*

AVOIDANCE PHASE

1. RECOGNIZE THE LOSS
- Acknowledge the death
- Understand the death

CONFRONTATION PHASE

2. REACT TO THE SEPARATION
- Experience the pain
- Feel, identify, accept, and give some form of expression to all the psychological reactions to the loss
- Identify and mourn secondary losses

3. RECOLLECT AND REEXPERIENCE THE DECEASED AND THE RELATIONSHIP
- Review and remember realistically
- Revive and reexperience the feelings

4. RELINQUISH THE OLD ATTACHMENTS TO THE DECEASED AND PREVIOUS ASSUMPTIONS ABOUT AND EXPECTATIONS OF LIFE

ACCOMMODATION PHASE

5. READJUST TO MOVE ADAPTIVELY INTO THE NEW WORLD WITHOUT FORGETTING THE OLD
- Revise the assumptive world
- Develop a new relationship with the deceased
- Adopt new ways of being in the world
- Form a new identity

6. REINVEST

*From Therese Rando, *Treatment of Complicated Mourning* (Champaigne, IL: Research Press, 1993).

luctant to have a service because doing so would "seem like we don't care." Without physical evidence of his death, they were holding onto hope that somehow he was alive. Several months later some of his belongings, weathered and torn from many storms, were discovered. Only then did the couple declare him dead and begin to grieve.

In addition to acknowledging the death, the mourner will often seek information about how the death occurred. The practical questions of when, where, and how the death occurred are asked until a satisfactory reason is found. This explanation may not be factual or realistic. A woman whose husband was killed in a motor vehicle accident concluded that his brakes failed whereas the police report indicated he had a blood alcohol level two times the legal limit. These initial explanations, even if unrealistic, serve to help the mourner acknowledge the death.

Some appear to accept the death and immediately begin to deal with the arrangements and needs of others. While aware of the loss, they put their own reactions aside so that they can do what must be done. Many men focus on the physical and emotional needs they perceive in others, wanting or believing they need to remain strong for loved ones. Parents of young children may also focus on the needs of the children and shelve their own reactions. This delay in personal response can initially be helpful to all involved. However, this way of coping, if prolonged, will interfere or prohibit the necessary work of grief.

Confrontation Phase

When a person gradually moves out of the avoidance phase because he or she acknowledges the loss, the intensity of grief increases. Now the basic facts are defined and the mourner is beginning to experience the implications of the loss and to feel the consequent pain. The entire body cries out, searching for the loved one, longing for a reunion.

When no reunion occurs, the mourner may be swept over by tides of sadness, sorrow, and anger.

The mourner is continually confronted with situations, expectations, social relationships, habits, and memories which involved the deceased. Each of these events requires the mourner to learn again what to expect and to learn how to relate as the deceased is not a present part of the relationship. The second process of grief, *reacting to the separation*, involves allowing ourselves to experience what we feel and think each time we are aware of the loss. Each time mourners are reminded of the loss they relearn what they want to know least, that the loss is real and permanent.

The realization of the loss leads some to bargain with God in the hopes of undoing the loss. "If only . . ." or "What if . . ." statements and pleas arise from the hope of being reunited with what has been lost.

The reactions to the separation vary between two extremes. On the one hand mourners may inhibit their reactions, suppress their feelings, limit thoughts about the loss, and generally live as if little is different. On the other hand they may focus on the loss, feel the anguish and sorrow, or be overwhelmed by the thoughts and feelings about the loss. This alternating between denial and acknowledgment is part of the coping process. The mourner eventually develops a psychological equilibrium between avoiding and approaching the loss.

When mourners allow themselves to experience their grief they discover that the loss is greater than just the death of the loved one. Also lost are the roles the deceased had, the hopes and dreams shared with them, and the expectations and habits that were shared. Mary, a widow after 29 years of marriage, shared that she felt as if a part of her had also died. The death of her husband was also the death of her partner, coparent and cograndparent, lover, and friend. Something as simple as not having anyone to talk to while driving the car was as much a part of the loss as anything else. These losses are called *secondary losses*. They may evoke reactions similar to the *primary loss* (in this example, the death of her husband). Oftentimes mourners are not immediately aware of their secondary losses and discover them over a period of months or years.

The third process, *recollecting and reexperiencing the deceased and the relationship*, paves the way for the journey of grief. Now that the reality of the loss is essentially accepted (although there will be times of question or hope that none of this is real), the only way to relate to the deceased is symbolically—that is, through the use of memory and imagination.

A man wrote that "in death, my family has made my father the saint I always had hoped for." But mourners need to remember the deceased in realistic terms. The good and the bad times, the endearing and the despised characteristics need to be recalled and accepted. There are thousands of emotional bonds to the deceased in our memory and each one needs to be adapted.

Feelings of shame, thoughts of guilt, and self-judgments may occur as the mourner is realistic about the deceased. The problems, unresolved conflicts, or the longing to be more fully loved by the deceased are now issues that can never be addressed with the loved one. These realizations, some of which are very unpleasant, need to be incorporated in the memory of the deceased.

Gradually mourners come to a broad awareness of their own reactions to the reality of the loss and to their memories, beliefs, understandings, and feelings regarding the deceased. Grief is the process by which the bonds between the mourner and the deceased are released. Each bond will be processed, each bond will be released.

Releasing the bonds that had connected the mourner with the deceased is the fourth process (*relinquish the old attachments to the deceased and old assumptions about and expectations of life)*. Letting go of the expectations that the deceased will be a part of daily living, a part of the future, a part of habits and expectations is necessary to adjust to what has been lost.

For some this process leads to a sense of helplessness and despair. The reality is that we are helpless to reunite with the deceased in our earthly existence. The reality is that the deceased will not drive into the driveway, share a special moment, or be there for the holidays. The cost of not adjusting to this truth is a loss of contact with reality.

The experience of helplessness can lead to anxiety, depression, and withdrawal. The more one holds onto what has been lost, the greater the investment of emotional energy, the greater is the potential for despair.

Loss is no less real for the Christian. Knowing that we have eternal hope (1 Thess. 4:13–14, etc.) does not change the reality of loss in the present. Many have found comfort in that Jesus wept upon hearing of the death of his friend Lazarus (John 11:35). Jesus knew how the story would end, that Lazarus would be part of a miracle demonstrating God's power. Yet his reaction was to cry out loud, expressing his grief.

Accommodation Phase

The ultimate goal of grieving is to learn to live with the reality of the loss and make necessary changes; to say goodbye to what has been lost and then live well in the present. We do not want to say goodbye, yet the pain of trying to hold onto what was lost is great. As we are able to become realistic with what we have lost (both primary and secondary losses) we can release the bonds of attachment.

The fifth process (*readjust to move adaptively into the new world without forgetting the old*) occurs as we let go. Life is different, who we are and the life we live is forever changed. We adopt new roles; for instance, being single, or a single parent, or as a member of the oldest surviving generation (in the case of the death of parents). We may have suffered a great loss, but end up becoming more because we do not lose who we were. We continue to move forward in life, growing and becoming more.

A new relationship is developed with the loss. Advice such as "put the past behind you" and "just get on with your life" ignores a critical need to have unity within ourselves, to have links between our past, present, and future. Emotional connections will remain with the deceased. These need not threaten relationships in the present. Rather, the new life situations, the new world lived in presently, involves relationships with both the past and present, each in their proper places. We do not forget nor do we stop caring about the loss as we near the end of the grief journey, we simply adjust.

Developing a new identity with our new roles, a new relationship with the deceased, and new perspectives on God and truth in general allows us to move into the final grief process. Finally, we can *reinvest*. We can take the attachments, the capacity to care and be cared for, to love and be loved, to be in relationship and apply them in new situations in new ways.

Approaching the End of the Journey

Our trek of mourning is for a season (Eccles. 7:2–4). What can we expect as we finish the journey? Let us first consider what we will not encounter. Grief is *not* resolved by

- forgetting or denial
- absence of pain
- idealizing what was lost
- acting as if the loss never happened

- pretending it doesn't matter
- trying to be in control
- despair or helplessness

Rather, grief resolution involves living well in the full awareness and acceptance of the loss. Thus, we can know we are nearing the end of the journey when we

- live in the truth
- experience a lessening of the pain
- accept the positive and negative characteristics of what has been lost
- accept the reality of the loss
- develop new relationships
- develop a realistic perspective of your relationship with the deceased
- grow and adapt
- have a new growing perspective on God, the world, and yourself
- become vulnerable again
- walk in faith with hope

We are forever changed by the journey.

Throughout the rest of our earthly lives we will have a relationship with what has been lost. We will have times when the pain returns, when we encounter a turn on our life's journey that holds an unresolved bond or tie to what has been lost. Such times may be holidays, anniversaries, and major life events such as a graduation, wedding, or birth. Someone who has departed may be remembered at any time on any day, or in one's dreams. Such experiences do not indicate that the grief journey was inadequate, but rather, reminds us that we are fearfully and wonderfully made (Ps. 139:14), that we are continually growing and adapting.

Grief's journey is resolved when mourners can be realistic about what was lost, about how the loss changed their lives, and be honest about their feelings and thoughts regarding all of this. They have come face to face with the multiple bonds and attachments they had and have released the pain in each. Finally they are able to live in the present with an appreciation and connection with what they have lost.

With the old attachment bonds released, we are able to invest our emotional, mental, spiritual, physical, and relational energies in the present. Grief's journey is not traveled on super highways but on twisting paths that wind through the many bonds, ties, and attachments we have developed through life. This is not the kind of journey we want to make—the passage is hard, painful work. Detours only delay the journey. The surprise near journey's end is the freedom and the opportunity to choose a new path, to invest in a new life. Then new journeys can begin.

5

Why Me?—
The Role of Anger

"Therefore I will not keep silent; I will speak out of the anguish of my spirit, I will complain in the bitterness of my soul."

—Job 7:11

I just want her back!" "Tell me this is just a nightmare." These and similar cries are uttered when we are confronted with the reality of serious loss. Death, for instance, is irreversible. We long to have the deceased rejoin us, even if for a moment. We want what was lost—and we can't have it.

On grief's journey we move through times of anger. For some people anger is their dominant response, while for others various emotions color their experience, although they are aware of their anger. Still others have great difficulty because they deny any experience of anger or feel ashamed of the fleeting moments of anger.

Anger is a part of the grief journey, a sometimes valuable part of the multiple reactions we have in our adjustment process. Feelings of anger can bring into our awareness

55

problems, violations, wrongdoing, or injustice. Anger cries out that something ought to change, that something is wrong and must be made right. In our heart of hearts we long to have the wrong corrected, the loss reversed. What can change, then, if we can't have what has been lost? We ourselves can change; we can be changed. The problem is, we don't want to change. The death of a loved one demands changes in all areas of life: in habits, expectations, and hopes.

How do you know when you are angry? You may notice some or all of the following:

- physical signs: tight muscles, upset stomach, headaches;
- subjective feelings: being upset, irritated, or distressed;
- thoughts: focusing on what is wrong, wanting to get back at someone;
- relationships: avoiding, picking fights, causing irritation or being irritated;
- resistance to change or acceptance.

We experience anger in situations that involve people or things that we care for or love.

Who's Responsible?

We are always trying to understand what happens to us and to find purpose and meaning in our lives. Great losses leave us feeling helpless, life seems out of control. At such times we experience a loss of motivation, emotional pain or numbing, and difficulties with thinking and memory. Depression and anxiety with sleep problems, changes in appetite, and a loss of interest in living can result.

In an attempt to avoid this, we often look for blame, or some place to put our anger and say "It's your fault!" Something as significant as the death of a loved one has to be for a reason, it must be someone's fault, it must have a purpose. This search may lead to blaming others, God, the person who died, or even ourselves.

Why do some blame themselves? Self-blame provides an answer to the question of responsibility. If I blame myself I am no longer helpless. Now I must be perfect and not let anything bad happen. It may be a way of "protecting" someone else from being responsible. Such attempts to maintain an idealized image of another person, to keep him or her "good," can backfire resulting in self-contempt, depression, and anger. Still others have learned that it is wrong to hold anyone responsible for an event or are ashamed of the anger they feel.

The Constructive Use of Anger

Scripture reveals that God is angry in the presence of evil or sin, and thus there are boundaries between him and wrongdoing. Consider Judges 2:20: "Therefore the LORD was very angry with Israel and said . . . 'this nation has violated the covenant that I laid down for their forefathers and has not listened to me.'" Disobedience, rebellion, slander, or any other sin evokes anger in God.

We too have anger when we experience a wrongdoing, a wrong event, or when things aren't the way they should be. Our anger can help us identify what needs to change, and it increases our energy and motivation. Anger is resolved when some kind of change occurs (external or internal).

There are times when we need to separate ourselves from what is hurtful, damaging, wrong, or sinful. Not all people are safe, not all desire what is good, and not all people act in love. Even those who may seem to want to help may be insensitive or hurtful. Most, if not all, mourners have stories of those who said the wrong thing, who, thinking they are being helpful, only elicited more pain. Remarks like "you should be over this by now," "it will be okay because you're pretty and can find another husband," or "God wanted her in heaven with him because he loves her so much" only hurt the mourner. These and similar responses by others, even when well intended, often elicit anger that causes mourners to distance themselves.

Myths about Anger

Anger is often misunderstood. The following list of commonly held misbeliefs about anger are offered to clarify the intended role of anger in our lives.

Anger Itself Is Sin

We need to remember that anger itself is simply an emotion—what we do with that emotion can be constructive or destructive. The Scriptures make many references to God's anger (cf., Num. 22:22; Deut. 1:34; Judg. 2:20; 2 Sam. 22:8; Job 42:7; Ps. 79:5). Jesus displayed anger on numerous occasions (e.g., Matt. 21:12–13; 23:13–39), always without sin.

The biblical teaching regarding anger is defined in Ephesians 4:26: "In your anger do not sin: Do not let the sun go down while you are still angry." We are responsible for how we act while we are angry and are admonished to resolve our anger.

If I Acknowledge My Anger, I'll Never Get Over It

Some fear that if they "take off the cork" their anger will never again be contained. The opposite is more often true since the direct expression of the anger will decrease the intensity of the emotion whereas blocking expression tends to magnify its intensity and prevent its resolution. Without holding someone responsible we cannot offer or accept forgiveness. The denial of our anger will actually encourage bitterness and block forgiveness.

All I Need To Do Is Express My Anger

On the other hand, it is a mistake to think that the expression of anger will automatically solve it. Research has demonstrated that mere anger expression often leads to only more anger. It is very important that the anger expression lead to the identification of what we are angry about and toward change.

If I Don't Think About It, My Anger Will Go Away

Some change must occur for anger to "go away" or to be resolved. We can alter our awareness of our anger, yet if the problem that is producing the anger has not been resolved, it will continue. Anger may be strongly influencing us even though we are unaware of its presence. It can lead to poor health, withdrawal from others, becoming "short" or irritable, or passive-aggressive behaviors.

My Anger Will Hurt Someone Else

Anger, like any emotional reaction, is an internal experience. What I do with my anger, how I act or treat others, may or may not produce a reaction in another person. While I am responsible for how I treat myself and how I treat others, I am not responsible for what they experience or how they treat me.

Accepting Anger Will Mean I Will Explode or Lose Control

Some people express anger in only one form: rage. Like other emotions, anger ranges from mild or low intensity (irritation) to high or great intensity (rage). We can learn to express anger in whatever intensity is appropriate for the situation. Being angry does not mean having to be in a rage.

Anger Is Always Irrational

Our anger at times is irrational. At other times, anger is a rational reaction to a wrong situation. Anger does not give us a definition of truth, but rather motivates us to find out what is wrong and change it. Anger can help us discover unrealistic expectations or beliefs that we hold. Working to resolve our anger can actually help us move toward what is true, right, and good.

My Anger Means I'm Not Coping Very Well, or that I'm Immature

Not necessarily. Anger is simply a response. We need to live in reality, accepting what is real, if we are to cope well. Maturity means being able to accept responsibility for ourselves and live in truth. The reality of living in a sinful world is that we do experience horrible losses, things do go wrong, injustices occur, and we do become angry.

My Anger Means I'm Not Trusting God

Again, not necessarily. Jonah was not trusting God's plan for the people of Nineveh when God confronted him with "Have you any right to be angry?" (Jon. 4:4). Yet God acknowledges righteous anger in other situations (Isa. 47) and at times reassured his people that he himself is angry at unrighteousness and evil.

It Is Wrong to Be Angry with Someone Who Has Died

The death of a loved one often evokes anger toward the deceased. This is difficult. The survivors may be angry that the loved one is no longer available for companionship, has "deserted" them, or left their personal effects in a mess. In other situations survivors may be angry about how the deceased died. Was there something the deceased did that contributed to their death? Were they somehow irresponsible or careless?

When someone dies we often suppress anger that would ordinarily be there. A couple who experienced the death of their teenage daughter in an auto accident were crushed to learn that she had alcohol in her blood. Had she lived, they said, they would have been very angry and would have suspended her driving privileges. However, they believed it was wrong to be angry now that she had died because "she had suffered enough already."

Anger is a personal reaction—it does not directly impact anyone else. It is not a punishment of another person (although many punish when they are angry). This couple was angry with their daughter, with themselves and each other (asking "where did we go wrong?"). They were angry she made a bad choice, a deadly choice (to drink and drive) and they were angry she had died. Only upon acknowledging their anger could they begin to heal and move past the anger.

Grief is the reaction of survivors—the deceased do not grieve. Even this truth can evoke anger. "How could you leave me to go through this pain so alone?" cried out a young widow. She needed to know, however, that her anger, and the anger of any survivor, does not impact the deceased. Rather, the anger responses are steps toward healing, toward the resolution of our grief.

Misuse of Anger

We can sin in our anger, as Ephesians 4:26 implies. It is not the emotion of anger itself that is the sin but rather our reaction to our anger. The choices we make regarding anger resolution will determine if we are benefiting from or misusing our anger. Below is a list of some of the ways we may misuse anger or resist resolving it.

Refusal to Resolve. We are designed with the ability to resolve our anger. The biblical mandate "Do not let the sun go down while you are still angry" (Eph. 4:26b) directs us to take action to make the necessary changes so that our anger can be released. The refusal to address and resolve our anger will produce bitterness against ourselves, others, or God.

Selfish Gain. We can use anger to take advantage of a situation. We feel more powerful, more in control when angry and may seek our own way through our anger.

Revenge. With the energy that comes with our anger, we may strike out to hurt someone who we believe has hurt us. In response to our own pain, we may want them to hurt as we do.

Denial of Anger. Denying, pretending, ignoring, or otherwise avoiding anger does nothing to change the situations that are causing the anger. Anger can be denied directly, even to the extent that one becomes angry when others question us about it. Less obvious denial strategies include busyness, not allowing time to think or feel, involvement in substitute relationships, or getting lost in caring or being cared for. Another way of denying one's anger is to embrace a victim role in which some people come to believe that "life will always be horrible." They focus on what happens to them as a means of denying their own reactions.

Illusion of Power. Many of the emotional reactions in grief leave us feeling weak, exposed, or vulnerable. Anger tends to energize us, giving us the experience of having power. At times mourners grasp their anger for relief from their pain. The attractiveness of bitterness lies in the power they experience as they identify with their painful circumstances. Still others may inadvertently conclude that they are only attended to by others when they are angry.

Holding onto Unrealistic Expectations. Our anger may be the result of demanding something we cannot have, such as the return of the deceased person. We may demand that our grief not hurt, that our grief end. Such common experiences are a part of the journey, they are not the destination. Such hopes become problems when they are embraced, when we hold onto them rather than continuing the journey.

All of these misuses of our anger serve to protect us from the pain of vulnerability. Loss exposes us to vulnerability, powerlessness, and pain. Bitterness, which is anger that has been left unresolved and has rotted, can lock us in a pattern of being stuck and feeling helpless. In such cases, grief cannot be resolved and healing will not occur.

Anger toward God

Our realization that something is wrong and our awareness that we can't make sense out of the loss may lead us to experience anger at God. If God is all powerful, how could he have allowed this loss? Doesn't God know how much this loss has hurt me? If God loves me, why didn't he do something? Why doesn't he do something now? I want God to take this pain away and he won't. Where is God? These and other questions and thoughts evoke anger.

Sometimes we are angry at God because we have nothing or no one else to be angry with. The loss seems so great, so wicked, so intense that it has eternal and ultimate implications. Experiences like rape, death of a loved one, an earthquake, and murder all transcend our understanding. Surely, this is where evil and good intersect. Why didn't good prevail?

For others, a simplistic view of God has left them vulnerable to feeling abandoned. A belief that God will only allow good things to happen to me implies that God has abandoned me when difficult times come. But God did not even treat himself in this manner; God the Son (Jesus) subjected himself to pain, suffering, even death. God has not promised us freedom from pain or difficult times.

Is anger at God dangerous? Is it wrong? What are we to do when we are angry at God? Stop and consider how a loving and just parent responds to the anger of his or her young child. The parent notices the child's anger, listens and cares for the child, but is not controlled or threatened by the child. The parent has a larger perspective, a greater capacity to understand, and many more choices. He or she does not wish to harm the child but rather to help the child understand, adjust, and accept the situation. This is a moment in which the parent can teach the child and the child can learn more about the parent and about reality. In a similar manner, God is not threatened by our anger, even though he wants us to grow beyond it. He wants us to move beyond the anger toward trust and acceptance.

What are we to understand about our anger toward God? A review of the Scriptures reveals four guiding principles.

1. Anger with God is not a desired reaction, is not intended to be an ongoing response, and may be one of the least constructive positions for us to be in.
2. It is naive to pretend believers never get angry at God.
3. If someone is angry at God, it is better to acknowledge it than to hide it and become bitter.
4. This anger may be a first step in accepting what is real and can be directed in more constructive ways.

Our challenge is to use this anger to change us and resolve the anger. Our view of God, of ourselves, and of life in general are challenged and changed on the journey of grief. At the end of the journey is the promise of a deeper and more realistic relationship with God and with others.

Children, Grief, and Anger

The anger of a child following a significant loss is similar to an adult's yet has unique features. Children are limited in their ability to think, understand, and make sense of their situation. They are dependent upon those around them. To differing degrees they attempt to please or take care of the adults in their world. Children are likely to blame themselves for any loss or bad event. Such self-blame may be clearly illogical to an adult but very real to the child.

To a child, the death of a parent or sibling may seem like abandonment, resulting in great fear and anger. Children need to know that they will be loved, cared for, and that they will be safe.

Children may act out or try to elicit the anger of parents who inhibit or deny their anger. They may attempt to care for the family by expressing anger, misbehaving, failing in school, fighting with siblings, or becoming either very distant, detached, or dependent and clinging. This may break the denial of the parents and bring about the parent's own grieving. Children may display their anger in direct or indirect ways as a cry for help, a plea for the family to adjust to the loss and meet current needs. They are not aware of these strategies but are trying to relate to their parents in a way that can meet their needs.

As children mature, their strategies for processing anger also develop. Losses that occur at a young age, such as the death of a parent of a preschooler, are likely to be reprocessed at each developmental stage. They may experience anger about the loss during middle childhood, during their teen years, and again in adulthood. Such anger does not indicate that their grief work was insufficient, but rather, helps them adjust to their life situation with each development.

Resolving Anger

Anger resolution is an active part of the grief journey. Listed below are choices that we can make to benefit from the anger we experience.

1. Accept that you are angry. Accept that God too is angry at things that are wrong and that our anger responses can help us to change and adjust to the loss.

2. Recognize the physical signs of your anger.

3. Identify what is causing the anger and direct your anger toward the relevant target, toward what makes you angry.

4. Identify what must change. In some situations you may need to change things around you. For example, you may need to take steps to stop secondary victimization from others. More frequently, we need to change something within ourselves. We may need to change an expectation, hope, habit, or demand. We may need to let go of what we can't have.

5. Take action to change. Express the anger with words and physical activity. In situations involving secondary victimization (when other people add hurt on top of hurt), we may need to talk with those involved and define boundaries or clarify expectations. In other situations, we may need to write out our anger, identifying what we are angry about, how we feel, and what we are going to do about it. Physical expression that is nondestructive may involve talking, yelling, crying, throwing stones, crushing cans, cutting wood, hitting a pillow, or any other expression that involves the whole body. We can benefit from talking out loud about our anger as we are physically active in anger expression.

6. Identify where forgiveness is indicated.

Children will often depend on their parents and other significant people in their lives to help them resolve their anger. The actions and attitudes displayed by the adults will greatly influence how children progress. The following suggestions are offered to parents and others who are caring for grieving children.

1. Teach the child about anger, letting him or her know anger is natural, that it can be used constructively, and that it can be resolved. Instruct and model that we are responsible for how we act when we are angry and that we have

choices about how we express and resolve our anger. Model anger ownership, expression, and resolution.

2. Teach the child to identify what the anger is about. Validate what is real. Help him or her link the anger to what is happening, what has been lost, or what is wrong. If you are also angry about this, let the child know.

3. Help the child identify what can change. Help him or her with options or opportunities.

4. Help the child discern what is and what is not his or her responsibility.

5. Practice personal responsibility and forgiveness in the family.

6. Respect the child's need for privacy and/or need to talk when angry. Respect the child's boundaries.

7. Remind the child of truth, hope, and unconditional love both from you and from God who will never leave him or her.

6

Where Is God in All This? Finding Divine Help

"The lowly he sets on high, and those who mourn are lifted to safety."

—Job 5:11

The Compassionate Heart of God

Serious loss in life can move us closer to God or seem like a gravity pulling us down and away. Sometimes it seems like both is happening. One reason is that, as creatures of emotion, we can have spells where some feelings simply make us feel alienated. Anger will do that and it certainly will if it turns into resentment or bitterness. When we feel hurt we feel vulnerable, even unprotected. Fear is also an alienating emotional experience. We may more sense the presence of danger or threat than rescue and deliverance. And then there is shame—a state of heart that is at its core one of disconnection and loneliness.

Fortunately, that is not the whole picture. Our emotions come and go, and many mourners will testify to the fact

69

that at their moment of loss they sensed their need for God more than any other time. They also sensed that he was present and available, as if the tearing away of the loss had left them alone with God and in his care more than they typically felt.

No matter what we sense or feel at any given time, we should rehearse the biblical truths communicated time and again about God's overflowing, compassionate heart.

- Lam. 3:32–33 Though he brings grief, he will show *compassion*, so great is his unfailing love. For he does not willingly bring affliction or grief to the children of men.
- Matt. 5:4 Blessed are those who *mourn*, for they will be *comforted*.
- Ps. 10:14 But you, O God, *do see* trouble and grief; you consider it to take it in hand. The victim *commits* himself to you; you are the *helper* of the fatherless.
- Isa. 60:20 Your sun will never set again, and your moon will wane no more; the LORD will be your *everlasting light*, and your *days of sorrow will end.*
- Matt. 12:20 A bruised reed he will not break, and a smoldering wick he will not snuff out.
- John 16:6, 20 Because I have said these things, you are filled with grief. I tell you the truth, you will weep and mourn while the world rejoices. You will grieve, but *your grief will turn to joy.*
- Heb. 4:15 For we do not have a high priest who is *unable to sympathize* with our weaknesses, but we have one who has been tempted in every way, just as we are —yet was without sin.

This is reality. God is love. He does not take delight in the tragedies and traumas of this fallen world. He has promised that he will remake the world as we know it into something better than our imaginations can conceive. And, in the meantime, his work among us includes giving us the grace to be able to get through times of loss, to be stronger afterward than we were before, and to be able to help others when we are ready to.

Things That Remain

Serious loss can feel like having something torn from you, or like the ground on which you were standing is shifting and changing, making you wonder what will come next. What can you count on in life? What is it that won't change? And what can you hold onto now that isn't going to disappear as well?

It is the *things that remain* that help us get through grief. That includes people who are important in our lives. While other people cannot replace our loss, nevertheless it is a good thing that they are there. They may not know exactly how they can help you in your mourning; they may make mistakes or be insensitive. It's a hard thing to try to understand what someone else is going through. Yet those people who have a genuine concern may be some of the most important resources a mourning person has.

Even more important, God himself remains. In our experience it may be hard to grasp that fact when someone or something central in our lives is suddenly gone. If the earth suddenly disappeared the moon's movement would be radically altered, it would even appear to spin out of control, a lost satellite. But the rest of the solar system would still be there; the sun and it's massive influence would remain unchanged, it's light and heat and energy still available.

Mourners do adjust to their losses, and that is why they mourn. The experience of loss makes them look at life from new perspectives. They realize that they had thought of some things as permanent and unchangeable, but they learned otherwise.

the wife whose husband only lived a year into the retirement that they had been planning for decades;

the young couple who assumed they could have children whenever they wanted but who faced serious infertility ten years into their marriage;

the fifty-year-old executive who was released from his company and can find no other interested in him;

the husband who learned of his wife's affair and her almost simultaneous filing for divorce;

the first-time parents who drive home from the hospital alone because their child was stillborn.

It is because everything in life is subject to change—everything—that the Bible talks as frequently as it does about God's unchangeable character.

- Mal. 3:6 I the LORD do not change. So you, O descendants of Jacob, are not destroyed.
- Ps. 33:11 The plans of the LORD stand firm forever, the purposes of his heart through all generations.
- Ps. 102:27–28 You remain the same, and your years will never end. The children of your servants will live in your presence; their descendants will be established before you.
- Deut. 31:8 The LORD himself goes before you and will be with you; he will never leave you nor forsake you. Do not be afraid; do not be discouraged.

After talking about the many things in life that are temporary and pass away, the apostle Paul said, "And now these three remain: *faith, hope and love*" (1 Cor. 13:13). If there is anything for us to seek out and hold onto when we grieve, it is these three. They are the spiritual moorings that keep us linked to God and grounded on a larger reality when someone or something has disappeared from our lives. They are truths that cannot be contradicted, gifts of God, characteristics of life that carry us through even traumatic events. They remain, and they help us remain.

Grief and Faith

Faith is belief. It is to hold onto something greater than yourself. During times of loss it is very important to keep referring back to the developed beliefs, the true beliefs, that have carried you along in life. Sudden or severe loss may shake up your beliefs, or you may discover that there was something important missing from your beliefs, but beyond all that, any faith that you had prior to the loss should be held onto and developed further.

Some people find themselves thrust back onto some of their most basic beliefs, remembering even childhood prayers that comforted then and comfort now.

Other people find that times of worship have a heightened importance. They know that something powerful is going on deep in their souls, and worship is a time when matters of the soul are respected and cultivated.

It is not unusual, on the other hand, for grieving people to find worship very difficult. Sometimes it is because they have a hard time being around other people, but it can also be just because their hearts feel raw—like they've been bruised and cut on the inside. They find themselves reacting to things that are said, feeling easily hurt or agitated. This is not very different from a person who has a broken foot and to whom any bump or pressure can feel excruciating. With time, the pain subsides, the injury heals.

Faith means stretching beyond yourself and getting your life moored to something more stable than yourself. Nobody is in a safe position being adrift in the currents of life, much more when those currents turn into the violent waves of a storm when serious loss occurs.

For those people whose only mooring was a person they lost, they will face a severe faith crisis. What they believed in was a person. But people change, people leave. Yet even then it's not too late to find a faith in something bigger than another person. God remains. People find new faith in him all the time.

The only reason faith can remain is that God remains. Faith in and of itself is the act of believing and trusting. The ropes that moor a boat alongside a stable and secure dock are meaningless in and of themselves unless there really is a dock to attach them to. So it really is not faith itself that saves—it is God.

Faith is not an elaborate structure that we build with our own insight and ability, a tower reaching to him so we can have access to him. Quite the contrary, God has come to us in the person of Jesus Christ. Knowing that we are unable to find truth ourselves, he came to teach us. Since we are unable to reform ourselves, he came to change us. And because we are unable to come up with the strength that we need to survive in a loss-filled world, he came to empower us.

For some people and at some times faith is a strong shout of strong belief; at other times it is a barely audible whisper for help. Either one will do, because faith is simply the opening between our needy existence and his super abundant grace. God can enter our lives through an opening the size of a garage door or the size of a keyhole.

Faith is built by listening to the voice of God. That's how all relationships of strong trust are built. The Bible, because it is God's own word to God's own people, is an expansive conversation between the God of heaven and the people he made to inhabit the earth. In it we find every conceivable kind of loss, real stories of real people who suffered such things as

- death and bereavement
- natural catastrophe
- betrayal
- loss of home
- loss of health
- loss of family
- loss of friendship
- loss of innocence
- loss of freedom

Instead of providing abstract spiritual truths, God saw fit to give a word that is clothed in real human experience. No matter what kind of loss you may experience, you can find the same thing in the Bible. In it we find scores of individual people who found ways to hold onto God when they went through times of severe loss. You may need some guidance as to what parts of the Bible to read when you are grieving, but don't be afraid to do it. The Psalms and the Gospel of John might be good places to read about why we go through what we do, and what God has done to help us.

Grief and Hope

In that short list from 1 Corinthians 13:13 ("these three remain, faith, hope, and love"), the next is hope. When we have experienced serious loss, looking to the future can be one of the hardest things for us to do. Facing tomorrow or even getting through today can look foreboding, let alone the years that lie ahead.

Yet hope is what allows us to face the future. It is the belief that we will be okay. It doesn't come to us out of thin air, and it is not wishful thinking. Some people tell others who are going through grief that they should just look on the bright side of things, but that is not hope. When people talk about "hoping for the best" it often doesn't get beyond a wish that the next roll of the dice won't be as fateful as the last one. But real hope is based on something—or rather, someone.

If faith in God is what supports us from behind (i.e., past experiences that convince us of his reality and his goodness), then hope is what pulls us ahead (i.e., into our future).

Grief is a matter of the soul—it touches us as deeply as any other experience. Numerous times in the Psalms the question arises: "Why are you downcast, O my soul? Why so disturbed within me?" To which the psalmist himself says: "Put your *hope* in God, for I will yet praise him, my Savior and my God" (Ps. 42:5, 11; 43:5). This kind of dialogue of the self with the self is exactly like the push and pull of grief on the soul—on the one hand a terrible inner aching and longing, on the other, a desire to survive, to be able to look to tomorrow and not be afraid.

God knows how crippling grief and trauma can be in our experience. He knows that mourners can feel so weak that they don't know how they can go on. And that is why many mourners find an extraordinary strength in God. The prophet Isaiah said:

> He gives strength to the weary and increases the power of the weak. Even youths grow tired and weary, and young men stumble and fall; but those who *hope in the LORD* will renew their strength. They will soar on wings like eagles; they will run and not grow weary; they will walk and not be faint (Isa. 40:29–31).

"Those who hope in the LORD." What does that mean? It means trusting that if he has done good things in the past, he will do so in the future; that if he has consistently been on the side of the right in the past, he will continue to be so in the future. It means believing that God does not change. God is really the creator of the future. He is a God of new beginnings, and sometimes a new future is molded with the best parts of the past. In other words God does not demolish the past to begin a new future; rather, he restores.

There are many ways that happens. In the case of losing someone close to you, the things that you valued in that person remain valuable, and nobody can take those values away from you; so also, the good memories you stored up in the past will go with you into the future. Those memories are more than just stored images or recorded information; they are a part of who you are, what shapes you today, and to that degree, those memories are not imaginary; they are living and they are real. In fact, it is not just that the good and substantial parts of the past *may* carry on in the future, they almost inevitably *will*.

If you have warm memories of someone you lost it takes great effort to suppress them. Some people try to do that as a way of avoiding pain, but it always fails. You can't evacuate yourselves of memories of the past, and you shouldn't try. That would only add loss on top of loss.

For the Christian there is another, fuller kind of hope that goes beyond all others: hope of eternal life. Now there are those who believe that when people die they are at the absolute end—irreparable loss, final silence. Most people living in most places at most times have believed otherwise. They have seen the incredible power of God-given life, the way that spiritual life transcends the merely material, and on that basis alone concluded that simple physical death couldn't possibly be the end. But there is more. There is the strong, wide, and continual voice of Scripture pointing to eternal life beyond the lives we know now.

Heaven is never described in the Bible as people sprouting wings, donning white robes, sitting on clouds as they hear or play an endless strain of harp music (a state of affairs that, to some, seems more torturous than paradisal). No, heaven is not the comprehensive loss of everything we have held near and dear in this life, but the complete fulfillment of it all. Though beyond our comprehension, the new heaven and the new earth the Scriptures point to is the fullest measure of real relationships, real beauty, real goodness. It is so because the departed believer has drawn closer to the creator of all good things than ever before.

For those who have a loved one die who displayed no apparent faith in God, the funeral can be especially somber. Many mourners who have faith find themselves rehearsing the fact that "the judge of the earth will do right" (Gen. 18:25), and that as mere mortals we are not in a position to make eternal judgments. It is not possible for the mourner to hold onto the person who has died; but it is entirely possible, and necessary, for the mourner to hold onto God.

It is an extraordinary joy to be able to celebrate the living faith of someone who died in the faith. Grief and mourning, tears and sobbing may still be there—these are not the denial of faith. But with faith is an other-worldly hope, a connection with the eternal, a link of future with future—that of the deceased who enjoys an improved existence in the presence of God, and the future of the mourners who know that God will carry them on in life.

And that is the explanation of this statement of the apostle Paul: "we do not grieve like the rest of men who have no hope." We will grieve loss (and so did the giants of the faith, and even Jesus himself); but it will not be a hopeless kind of grief.

Hope endures. And it helps us endure.

Grief and Love

"These three remain, faith, hope, and love. But the greatest of these is love." 1 Corinthians 13 also says, "[Love] always protects, always trusts, always hopes, always perseveres. Love never fails." There are, of course, many empty and half-hearted expressions of love. Sometimes people fall short of the love they claim to offer.

Yet where there is real love it has an incredible enduring power and value and for that reason it is able to help the mourner get through grief. Love does not dissipate because of distance. It is not shattered because of tension or temporary conflict. It perseveres when there are difficulties. When loss occurs, love is not ruined. You may lose a loved one, but not lose the love. Death cannot bury memories of love. Love is what turns memories from mere mental data into warm, living remembrances. Like faith and hope, love is one of those experiences of life that remains. It is another mooring available when you feel like a storm surge is pressing hard against you. Like faith and hope, the reason love remains is because it is one of the links that we have with God.

Real love is essentially a spiritual resource. It is not borne of human invention and initiative. The Bible teaches that we are capable of love only because it is who God is.

> Love comes from God. Everyone who loves has been born of God and knows God. Whoever does not love does not know God, because God is love. . . . No one has ever seen God; but if we love one another, God lives in us and his love is made complete in us (1 John 4:7, 8, 12).

When God "showed" himself to Moses in the Old Testament, God's own words describing his own being centered on his love:

> The LORD, the LORD, the compassionate and gracious God, slow to anger, abounding in love and faithfulness, maintaining love to thousands, and forgiving wickedness, rebellion and sin (Exod. 34:7–8).

It's no wonder that real love has such enduring value. It would not be an exaggeration to say that love is who God is; it is why he made us; it is the substance of good human relationships; it is the reason that life is a process of gain as well as loss. If we are made in the image of God (and the Bible says we are) and if God is love (and the Bible says he is), then love is one of those qualities overlapping the divine and the human.

If we did not love we would not hurt when we lose. And the opposite is true: if you want to protect yourself from any sense of grieving, if you want to avoid ever having to be a mourner, then don't let yourself love. But if you do, you will cut yourselves off from who God is and who mankind is intended to be. You may avoid the sense of loss, but only because you've caused yourself to lose what is most important in life.

How do we find God's help when we grieve? We ask him to show us what it is that remains even in the face of devastating loss. And much does remain. We ask him to strengthen our faith, lengthen our hope, and deepen our love.

When Jesus himself faced the loneliness and desolation of his own imminent death he asked several of his friends to abide with him, to remain. His words, embellished by a hymn writer, have often been sung as a prayer by needy people asking God himself to remain:

> Abide with me, fast falls the eventide;
> The darkness deepens; Lord with me abide!
> When other helpers fail and comforts flee,
> Help of the helpless, oh, abide with me.

7

What Can I Do to Help Myself?— Strategies for Self-Care

"Carry each other's burdens, and in this way you will fulfill the law of Christ . . . for each one should carry his own load."
—Galatians 6:2, 5

Grieving is an inner process, a personal journey; but it can be helped along greatly if the mourner is aware of many practical issues. There are so many questions mourners face: should I seek out other people? do I change my work patterns? should I try to go on as if nothing has happened? would I be better off if I moved at this time? should I allow myself to cry? do I lessen my responsibilities? There are ways mourners can help themselves get through the house of mourning in a constructive, healthy way. We will consider issues of health, relationships, lifestyle, spiritual life, and others. Much of what is covered in this chapter is aimed at those facing bereavement through death, but the same principles can apply to any kind of serious time of grief.

Guarding Your Health

Deep mourning is not only a spiritual and psychological experience, but affects one's physical life as well. This should come as no surprise since our inner and outer lives are so woven together. Recall from Chapter 2 that a grief response may include in the initial phases reactions of fatigue, confusion, and having low energy. When grief is complex or long term and thus complicated, other factors might come into play like depression that have great physical effects.

Common sense dictates that one keep to healthy patterns of eating and sleeping as much as possible. Mourning can cause a person to lose appetite or develop unusual patterns of overeating as a way of covering over pain. Though some variation from usual patterns is to be expected, it is dangerous for undereating or overeating to be a long-term trend.

So also, sleeping may be affected during mourning; there is nothing unusual about that. But if lack of sleep or effective sleep becomes a long-term problem, then it should be dealt with. A combination of altered eating and sleeping patterns with feelings of hopelessness or despair may point to the onset of depression. The advice of a psychologist, psychiatrist, or physician should be sought.

Someone in mourning may not feel like exercising. But here too there can be a danger in lethargic behavior over an extended period of time. Something as simple as walking can have great benefits to overall physical and mental well-being.

Some people may be tempted to use drugs or alcohol as a way of dulling their sense of mental, emotional, and spiritual anguish. The signs of an abusive use of substances include: drinking alone, recurrent use that interferes with responsibilities at work or at home, continued use in spite of the expressed concern of others, taking risks, etc. If a mourner realizes he or she has slipped into such abuse, then he or she should immediately confide in someone trusted and truthful, and seek professional help, at least on the level of consultation.

One's own physical health can be the furthest thing from one's mind in the case of, let us say, the death of a loved one. Indeed, the concerns that others have that the mourner eat regularly, sleep well, and get out more may seem petty and trivial. Yet the mourner needs to tell himself or herself that there is a simple truth here; and that it is important to observe basic standards of health.

And there is another point to be made here. Sometimes those going through grief feel as though there would be something wrong in taking care of themselves. There is a sense of shame in going on with life when someone close to you dies—after all, it could have been you; maybe it should have been you (some people think). The phenomenon known as "survivor guilt" can cause a person to neglect his or her own welfare. Yet it is obvious that for the mourner to decline and suffer is no way to honor the deceased; and, in virtually all instances, it would violate the wishes of the deceased.

Lifestyle Issues

When serious loss occurs there will be a process of adjustment going on inside the mourner, (which is grief itself), and those adjustments may very well affect the lifestyle of the mourner in areas like the pace of life, levels of responsibility, and decision making. Expectations are a major issue. When we mourn we may place on ourselves all kinds of expectations, and the people we know will have their own expectations. Some want the mourner to go on as if nothing has happened, perhaps thinking that the best road to healing is to get right back into the prior way of life. But an opposite set of expectations may be imposed as well— the assumption that the mourner is an invalid who should alter his or her lifestyle into one of isolation and passivity until he or she feels better. Neither of these extremes is likely to be helpful.

First, there is the issue of pace. Mourning may feel like walking through molasses—everything takes longer, seems to require more thought and more effort; you don't get done as much as you used to, and may even feel less valuable as a result. Grief taps the energy of a person. Loss is like a wound. In today's fast-paced society we sometimes get a certain momentum going that carries us through a rapid fire string of activities every day. There is no doubt that loss and grief will alter that. Mourning is a time of reflection, and there needs to be time and energy for it.

Then there is the issue of responsibilities. Mourners need to understand as do people around them that they may need to ease back into their previous responsibilities. Where it is possible, it is good to return to work gradually. Of course employers have different standards for what they allow (sometimes standards that profoundly underestimate the effects of loss). While you may get time off work if you lose a parent, that doesn't mean you will if you lose your best friend, which in some circumstances could be a more grievous loss.

Responsibilities for housework and maintenance, bill paying, childcare, may be areas where the assistance of friends or family members may be called for. It is nothing to be ashamed of to ask for such help. And it is not realistic to think that other people will automatically step in and offer specific forms of assistance.

Sometimes a serious loss necessitates some unexpected decisions. A widow, for instance, may need to decide to get a job or a different job, learn new skills, perhaps even move to a different house or apartment or to another state or city. These are major decisions that are a consequence of loss and they need to be approached very carefully and cautiously. More than ever, in such circumstances mourners need to actively seek good advice from people who know them well, and from legal, medical, or other professionals as need be.

Too much change too quickly is not good. If there is no necessary reason to sell the house, move to a new community, sell the business, get a different car, etc., there is reason to hold off on such decisions. The mourner may feel like distancing himself or herself from the things that remind him or her of who was lost, but making rapid changes may not reduce pain at all. In fact, it can add loss on top of loss.

Some of the seemingly simplest changes can be the hardest. When, for instance, do you change the room or get rid of the clothes and other personal belongings of someone who has died? On the one hand it may be a sign that adjustments are not being made if all physical belongings are held intact for more than a year; but the other extreme may not be helpful either—abruptly getting rid of everything. It is good to keep some physical objects as mementos so that the mourner remembers that the past is important and that not even death can obliterate a relationship.

It is not uncommon for those who lose a spouse to find a new companion, perhaps quite quickly (this is especially true for widowers). There may be any number of reasons why that new person suddenly steps into the gap, but it should be recognized that you cannot take a shortcut around grief by finding a substitute. If there is a new relationship that is wholesome and viable, that's wonderful; but any decision for it to be permanent must be made on objective grounds, and not out of a sense of emotional supply and demand. There needs to be time. The one-year mourning period of widows or widowers may now be regarded as old-fashioned and artificial, but there is wisdom in customs of the past where it was socially acknowledged that those who grieve do spend time in "the house of mourning."

Support from Other People

It can hardly be stressed enough how important other people are in the healing process of grief. Sadly, it is also true that other people can add considerable complications to mourning. On balance, however, it is best to look for connections with others. What follows are suggestions for how to find the right kind of support from the right kind of people.

Don't Be Afraid to Ask

If a person in need does the best job he or she can to convince others that there is no need, then personal support will be stopped before it has begun. People going through grief need to be aware of their own attitudes toward personal need. Some have grown up in an environment that was very stoic. The way you deal with personal pain is to suck it up, and not to, in some (supposedly) shameful way, show your neediness or vulnerability. Others may be afraid of imposing on other people. They may even have an instinct to take care of other people when they themselves are the ones in obvious need (and, unfortunately, there are other people who will take advantage of that). Yet none of this is a very fair and mutual arrangement, and healthy relationships depend on mutuality. If you are willing to help someone else in need, then make sure you allow them the opportunity to help you.

Realize That You May Need to Express Specific and Concrete Needs

It would be nice if those around the grieving person would think carefully and creatively about what they could do to be helpful, and then offer it. Some people are insightful and concerned enough to say, "I would like to offer to come and cut the grass on Saturday mornings," or "You pick a day when I can take care of your kids for the whole day so you can go and do whatever you want," or "I'll rearrange my schedule so I could go with you to talk to the funeral director—that is, if you want me to." What is more likely is that well-meaning people will say something like, "You just let us know if you need anything." They may feel awkward, not knowing whether it's an imposition to offer anything more, not knowing whether you want someone around or want people to keep their distance.

Yet you may really need help. Maybe you need assistance with funeral preparations, or with taking care of practical things in the days following a funeral. Many people need help with settling an estate or making good decisions because of changes that have been imposed upon them. There are people who are willing to help. What they need is a specific and concrete request.

Mourners may worry about rejection: what if I ask for help, and no one is willing? That risk becomes less if you turn to people who you have a pretty good idea have a basic concern for you; and if you bear in mind that if someone cannot come through, it may be circumstantial, and it certainly does not reflect poorly on you.

Keep Realistic Expectations

When people are deeply grieving they want the pain to go away, the gap to be filled in. Oftentimes mourners will find that time spent with friends and companions can lift their spirits, make them think about other things; but then, when they are alone again, they feel the emptiness. They may think that next time they will avoid the social contact because it is too painful to feel the letdown. On the whole, however, it is better to have those moments of the fresh air of companionship than not. Over time, it will become easier to sense the benefits of being with other people. It will begin to feel normal again.

The one thing that will not be helpful is to expect other people to be able to fill in the space left by the loss. To use an analogy, if the family dog is killed a parent may be tempted to comfort the children by promising to get them another dog, to which they will inevitably react that they don't want a new or different dog—they just want their old friend back. Now with the passage of time it just may be that getting a new puppy is healing, but not a substitute for saying goodbye to old Spot.

Mourners may have unrealistic expectations, but even more likely is that they will be imposed upon by other people. Well-meaning friends can make the mistake of trying to get a widow or widower into a dating relationship in an untimely or awkward way. They may expect that getting back to work a week or so after the funeral will make all that grief melt away. Expectations during a season of grieving can make the process complicated and difficult. Like a river that cuts it's own course, the process of grieving must take place naturally and at it's own pace.

Seek People Who Understand

When we suffer loss one of the things our hearts long for is someone else who can understand. It's amazing how healing that contact, even in brief conversations or knowing looks, can help the person who is grieving. Not everyone is capable of understanding and empathy. The grieving person may need to actively seek them. They are often found outside the circle of previously known friends and family members. Sometimes it's a pastor or a counselor; other times, it's a friend of a friend with whom a simple phone conversation can be reassuring or enlightening.

Support groups can be tremendously helpful in dealing with grief. They are composed of people sharing the same kind of loss, and their agenda is usually very simple: to provide mutual understanding and support. Some may meet for just a few weeks, others are long term. Some are structured, others are simple in format. The hosts may be churches, hospitals, mental health clinics, or others. There are support groups for many situations, including

- new widows or widowers
- parents who lose a child
- children who lose a parent
- parents who have a stillborn child
- people who lose their jobs
- terminally ill people
- people working through the grief of chronic illnesses

It is sometimes difficult for those in grief to have the courage, trust, or energy to seek out such resources. Other people can help by making phone calls, getting details, even going with the grieving person to register. The grieving person should tell himself or herself, however, that there is nothing to lose by trying it, and that multitudes of people would testify that they found more healing by going to a support group than they ever expected to find.

One excellent way to find understanding is to read books written by insightful and compassionate people about the kind of loss you are going through. Granted, it's not the same thing as a warm hug or a face-to-face conversation, but the advantage of seeking such resources is that you will find specific insights to help you cope with and grow through the particular kind of grief you are facing, be it the death of a child, grieving someone who committed suicide, recovering from divorce, or a multitude of other circumstances.

When Grief Gets Complicated

"Uncomplicated grief" is that normal difficult process of adapting to a change resulting from loss. It is grief the way grief is supposed to work, not easy, not pleasant, but necessary.

There can develop complications, however, that impede the progress of grief. They prevent emotional and situational adjustments, and thus the grieving slows down or even gets stuck. It is when grief becomes delayed, or chronic, or exaggerated. The mourner feels overwhelmed and may behave in ways that only make it harder to get through the grief.

Two of the most common manifestations of "complicated grief" are depression and anxiety.

Depression

Grief itself is not depression. This point is extremely important. Some people think of grief and depression as the same thing because both include sadness and pining, feeling lost and in pain, being less active and less motivated. When a person is grieving these reactions are normal. (Indeed, their absence is abnormal where serious loss has occurred.) Grief is not a problem to be fixed but a process to be lived out. A mourner may speak in terms of "feeling depressed," by which is meant a pervasive sense of sadness. Depression in the full sense, however, goes much further.

Depression is when someone is so overwhelmed that his or her personal life is disrupted and shows such signs as poor appetite, loss of weight, difficulty in sleeping, a sense of worthlessness or hopelessness or despair, or even suicidal thoughts. When depression hits a person shows signs of not coping well at all. It is not just having a "bad day" here and there, but when every day is difficult to survive. When people grieve the world may look harsh and empty, but when they move into depression they look at themselves as part of the bleakness.

The grieving person may focus on the loss that has occurred, but when depression sets in there is a more generalized sense of distress. In a similar way, the mourner may have a sense of anger toward the cause of the loss, but when a mourner becomes depressed his or her anger becomes much more diffuse, or even directed at the self. He or she will tend to withdraw from other people rather than accept their offers of comfort or assistance, or may even be irritated or agitated.

Here, then, are some signs that indicate that grief may have become complicated by depression, and thus require other forms of assistance:

- physical disturbances such as weight loss or gain, loss or increase of appetite, insomnia;
- a sense of despair or hopelessness about life;
- a sense of personal worthlessness, shame, or no self-esteem;
- an inability to function in your normal environments (on the job, at home, etc.) due to excessive crying or pervasive sadness;
- suicidal thoughts;
- when these signs reoccur some time after the loss occurred;
- when these signs become a regular pattern for six months or longer.

Because serious depression can be a personally devastating experience, it warrants seeking professional help via the services of a psychologist, psychiatrist, or other competent therapist. The good news is that depression is treatable. Many people have walked through the dark valley of depression stemming from their grief, and with the right spiritual, psychological, and medical assistance, have come through the other side.

Anxiety

With all of the complex things happening during a time of mourning, it may not be noticed that the person has a significant problem with anxiety, which can pave the way for depression. Some anxiety is normal whereas serious anxiety may be experienced as panic attacks, phobic (fear) reactions, or a general sense of anxiety about everything.

A panic attack is when a person senses a loss of control, great distress, impending doom, and physical arousal (e.g., a racing heart, accelerated breathing, or excessive muscle tension). Phobic reactions are when someone has an unusual fear or avoidance of an object, person, or place. It may be fear of a room in the house, having dinner with the family, or having contact with other people. Anxiety can also come out as obsessions or ruminations.

In any case, here too the mourner needs something more than the passage of time to get past the difficulties. Racing anxiety stands in the way of the internal adjusting process of grief and will only prolong it. Professional help may include the development of skills to bring down the level of anxiety or medical treatment.

Complicated grief needs to be taken seriously. Whether the problem is serious depression, anxiety, or physical disturbances, the mourner does not need one profound problem added on top of another.

Grief may become complicated when a loss in the present is the catalyst for grieving over losses of the past. Unresolved losses can have a cumulative effect. If one experiences very strong or complicated grief for something that doesn't seem to warrant it, one should investigate whether the present loss is tying into incomplete grief from the past.

Though grief comes to us as a kind of imposition (because none of us wants to lose something or someone important to us), that does not mean that we are helpless. In the past two chapters we have considered some of the ways we can access God's help for the profound spiritual needs that grieving produces, and the ways we can help ourselves by linking ourselves to sources of strength and stability outside ourselves. The help is there. We are not alone.

8

Beyond Grief— The Experience of Trauma

"A time to tear and a time to mend"

—Ecclesiastes 3:7

In the next two chapters we turn to an experience that goes far beyond the normal experience of grief. All significant losses produce some kind of grief; but only some kinds of loss are so jarring and damaging that we call them trauma.

They are the kinds of losses that are so overwhelming, so painful, so extreme, that they exceed our ability to cope. Like the psalmist, we cry out, "My soul is in anguish. How long, O Lord, how long?" (Ps. 6:3). We may search for a cause, for meaning, for some good to come out of all of the pain. Ultimately, we are alone with our own experience, with ourselves. "This has happened to *me*" we conclude. My life is different, forever changed. I am different. Why has this happened? Who am I now?

The losses of trauma may be so intense that body, mind, and soul seem devastated; they are profoundly changed both in the short term and in the long term. Traumatized people are on grief's journey, albeit a severe one, complicated by troublesome, frightening, and disturbing experiences.

Understanding Trauma

Created in God's image, we have a deep need to understand, to make sense out of what happens to and around us, and to develop meaning in life. Trauma devastates our ability to make sense out of what is happening. In the aftermath of trauma the survivors are often unable to describe to themselves or others what has or is happening to them—although coming to understand what has happened and how it has impacted them will directly affect their ability to cope.

Trauma is the experience of something shocking happening to a person (physically or psychologically) that causes some kind of inner injury and affects the person's ability to function in normal ways. Trauma is a combination of three factors: (1) the events that happen, (2) the effects on a person, and (3) the person's ability to cope with the events. Something is traumatic when horrible events overwhelm a person's ability to cope with these events, resulting in psychological, emotional, social, spiritual, and physical wounds. The effects of trauma can last a lifetime.

The experience of trauma so overwhelms our ability to make sense out of the event that we actually think and solve problems differently than before. Typically, adults transform their experiences into some form of symbolic code (images, logic, language) and store the information in memory. Present situations are understood by accessing memory and interpreting the present in light of past experiences or knowledge. A traumatic experience is outside the scope of our past experiences—is outside the scope of what we can symbolically process. We just have no words to describe such a horrible new thing. At the moment of trauma we are unable to symbolically represent reality to ourselves. This experience is extremely distressing, overwhelming, and threatening. At such times we feel powerless, helpless, and vulnerable.

What Makes Something Traumatic?

All traumatic events involve loss but not all losses are traumatic. A situation is traumatic when a person is rendered helpless and in great perceived danger, when injury or death have either occurred or appear (to that person) likely to occur. Traumatic events involve events that significantly threaten a person's safety or life.

Normal losses in life are not considered trauma. For example, the loss of a job, a child marrying and moving to another state, or the death of a parent will likely have a great impact on a person. These losses, however difficult to cope with, are typically not considered traumatic as they are within the scope of common human experience. However, these events may be traumatic if the person is already so overwhelmed by life's demands that they seem a great threat to the person's safety. Trauma refers to events outside the normal scope of daily living.

The intensity of trauma or the degree of damage an event causes in a person's life is determined by both (a) the characteristics of the event, and (b) the individual person's capacity to cope with the event. Some events, such as the death of one's family in a fire, having been sexually abused as a child, or having been raped are traumatic to all people. Trauma may occur even if the direct harm did not occur to you but you observed the event (vicarious trauma). A person who witnesses a brutal killing may be traumatized and display similar reactions as one who had actually experienced direct physical violence.

Natural catastrophes, such as floods, violent storms, volcanic eruptions, landslides or avalanches, earthquakes, fires, tornadoes, and hurricanes, are often experienced as traumatic. Ordinarily we expect our environment to be safe, stable, and predictable.

As traumatic as natural disaster can be, human-made catastrophes appear to be more devastating. The negative effects of the trauma are likely to be greater if the disaster was caused by people, greater yet if the trauma was an intentional act.

Wars traumatize both soldiers and civilians exposed to the harsh realities of the killing and destruction. The incidence of violent crimes has increased over 500 percent in the last 30 years as these acts have become more brutal and depersonalized. Most crime is not perpetrated by strangers but family members. Research estimates indicate that approximately one-third of children in the United States are significantly physically and/or sexually abused. Still others have been purposefully tortured for the pleasure, political causes, or beliefs of others. The human capacity to harm and abuse others, evident from the first human family, perpetuates traumatization.

Another form of trauma is automobile and motorcycle accidents that kill as many people annually as the total number of Americans killed in Vietnam. Industrial accidents, diving accidents, and other accidents in transportation (train, airplane, bus, etc.) may also be traumatic.

In general, the effects of a traumatic event are greater under the following circumstances:

- the trauma is caused by humans;
- there is a significant threat (or perceived threat) to life;
- there is exposure to death, dying, or destruction;
- a person (or persons) of emotional significance is (are) harmed or lost;
- the trauma happens suddenly and unexpectedly;
- it is ongoing;

- it results in displacement or disruption in one's home community;
- there is little social support;
- there is a potential for recurrence;
- moral conflict is elicited by the events;
- the traumatized person had a role in the event.

In identifying these factors, it must be remembered that how any given event impacts any specific person is dependent not only on the event but also on the characteristics of the person.

The Effects of Trauma

Many people who are traumatized make a good adjustment to life. After the trauma they continue with their daily activities, adjusting well to life's changes. For others, their lives are never the same. Great changes have occurred in their relationships with themselves, others, and God. For both groups of trauma survivors, changes have occurred in how they respond to stress, how they react (physically, emotionally, mentally, spiritually) when they encounter perceived demands or threats.

Traumatic experiences produce what many researchers call "speechless terror." Being overwhelmed by the circumstances, unable to protect or get away, traumatized people are unable to form words to describe what is happening to them or how they feel. They are helpless. Intense emotions interfere with their ability to think, solve problems, or even process memory in their typical fashion. They become lethargic, unmotivated, and believe that they are helpless in many areas beyond their traumatic experience. Depressive and anxious symptoms are common. These patterns may result for a long time; for many they are evident for the rest of their lives. Multiple research programs have demonstrated that the experience of trauma can permanently change brain and hormonal functioning.

"It Never Goes Away"

It is so ironic that the worst moment of life is relived in different ways over and over. Memories of the trauma can intrude at any moment, break into awareness without any warning. People may feel as if they are again in the trauma experience and although their eyes tell them they are elsewhere, the trauma seems very real and current. For a brief time it is all happening again.

Reexperiencing the trauma is not limited to thoughts, memories, or feelings. The body may respond as if the trauma is current. The heart may race, sweating become profuse, muscles tense, and even trembling may occur. Such physical symptoms may occur with or without conscious awareness of the trauma.

Sleep may provide no relief. Nightmares in which the event is replayed are commonly experienced by those who have been traumatized. The dreams may seem real or symbolic. For some the dreams seem like a complete event or story, while for others they may be a single physical sensation or a sense of being back in "that place," i.e., where the trauma occurred. Many experience being startled to alertness, waking confused with a racing heart, fear, and sweating.

Feeling out of control, and thus in constant danger, many who have been traumatized become hypervigilant, or sense they are always on guard, always searching for signs of danger. Anything that symbolizes or reminds a traumatized person of the trauma may produce fear. Others may perceive that they are hypersensitive or overreactive. Even seemingly little events may produce a strong reaction.

All of these intrusive memories contribute to a sense of helplessness including a sense that one cannot control one's own mind. When we are confronted with helplessness we attempt to define why this is occurring. Why did this happen? What caused this? If we conclude that the cause was due to something outside of ourselves, was temporary, and was specific to a situation unlikely to reoccur, we are less likely to experience or maintain a sense of helplessness. However, if we conclude the cause of the trauma was due to ourselves, was stable or ongoing, or was global and likely to reoccur, we are likely to experience continued helplessness.

In such a situation many attempt to regain a sense of control, to minimize their sense of helplessness and vulnerability, by blaming themselves. They may think "if I blame myself, then I have some control on minimizing the likelihood of future occurrences and may be able to derive some meaning of the situation. To regain safety, I have to make sure I never do that again." It is common for abused spouses to blame themselves for the violence they experienced or for survivors of accidents to blame themselves for the death of someone else. Even the rape victim, the child who was sexually abused, or the person who experienced the death of a loved one often blame themselves for these tragedies. Our need to sense that we have control or influence in our world is a central human characteristic.

"What's Happened to My Body?"

Trauma changes people in not just psychological ways. The physical body is affected, with many of the effects being long term. Exposure to even one traumatic event can permanently alter one's neurological and hormonal systems; in other words, the very function of the brain is affected. Traumatized individuals react differently to stress. The symptoms of such changes include:

- exaggerated startle response, especially to sound or touch;

- hyperarousal: general body tension and chronic flight or fight response, including muscle tension, increased heart rate and blood pressure, increased sweating, dry mouth;
- hyperreactivity (i.e., exaggerated responses) to situations associated with the trauma;
- hyperreactivity to neutral situations;
- hyperreactivity to sounds;
- emotional hyperreactivity to things that remind one of the trauma;
- emotional numbing, restricted emotional experiences, or a decrease in the positive and negative emotions with most of life experienced as neither positive nor negative;
- loss of interest or excitement in things that used to be enjoyed;
- difficulty with relaxation;
- difficulty with sleep;
- difficulty with sexual functioning;
- impaired immune system functioning (resulting in increased illnesses);
- memory disturbances;
- difficulties with problem solving, concentration, and information processing;
- intrusive memories or flashbacks of the trauma;
- decreased tolerance for stress;
- increased use of alcohol, drugs, or other substances that provide relief from pain;
- avoidance of anything that may remind one of the trauma;
- avoidance of social situations.

Much of what we know about the effects of trauma on our bodies has come from research with animals, which has demonstrated that both the biochemistry and actual brain structures may be altered following trauma. Animals who have been exposed to trauma display increased reactivity, impaired learning and coping abilities, gastric ulcerations, and impaired immune system functioning.

Childhood trauma appears to have significant effects. Children are born with minimally developed brains; early life experiences help shape the maturing brain. Animal research has demonstrated that trauma changes how the brain develops, both physically and in how the animal copes with life. Other research has shown that people who experience trauma as children are more likely to be depressed or anxious as adults; and still other research has shown that the physical changes that occur to children who are traumatized are long lasting and evident during their adult years.

What is happening that accounts for these changes? Research in recent years has begun to answer this question.

Several systems influence the body's response to dangerous situations. The noradrenaline system, for instance, modulates the activation of the body for emergencies, our "flight or fight response." Heart and respiration rates increase, the muscles under the skin draw tight to prevent excessive wounding (producing "goose bumps"), and blood flow is redistributed with flow decreased in the hands, feet, and internal organs and increased in the skeletal muscles and brain. Pupils dilate, blood coagulates more quickly, and the senses become focused on potential danger. The brain has more blood (and oxygen) and functions very efficiently, discarding irrelevant information in favor of anything related to danger. These reactions are normally temporary effects during the alarm phase of a stress response. People who have been traumatized may chronically experience an excessive amount of this activity. It is no wonder their lives are affected. Their bodies are constantly telling them there is some imminent danger.

Trauma appears to reset several hormonal systems, including cortisol, epinephrine and norepinephrine, vasopressin, oxytocin, and endogenous or naturally occurring opioids. These hormones are involved in regulating our body's tension, memory encoding, and anxiety. They increase one's perception of fear, vulnerability, or danger.

Natural opioids, the automatic and natural chemicals released in response to pain or fear, impact our experience of painful sensations and emotions. These chemicals affect the brain the same as heroin. Trauma can greatly increase their production, resulting in emotional numbness, memory impairment, apathy, nightmares, nervousness, and mood swings. Intense emotionality involving intense expression of anger and fear may also be a product of this activity. High secretion of these chemicals is associated with self-stimulation, risk taking, crisis seeking, and the interpretation of events as dangerous. A traumatized person may become addicted to his or her own natural opioids and engage in dangerous or stressful crisis behaviors to increase the release of these chemicals. Others self-medicate through the use of alcohol or other substances.

During the last twenty-five years researchers have linked many of the psychological impairments produced by trauma, such as memory disturbances, flashbacks, nightmares, apathy, emotional numbing, alcohol and substance abuse, and self-stimulating risk taking, with physical, neurophysiological, and hormonal changes. The posttrauma brain may function differently than it had previously.

"I Don't Remember . . ."

The experience of trauma may disturb memories, thought processes, and the ability to solve problems and understand other life situations. Here is the person who cannot remember the first fifteen years of his or her life, or the combat veteran who can't recollect his tour of duty. Initially, the thinking processes of the traumatized person are focused on basic survival as all attention is directed toward sustaining one's life and coping with what must be done. These experiences are so overwhelming that thinking processes and memory do not function in a normal manner.

In normal situations, our memory functions to relate present experiences with past experiences. As adults, our experiences are transformed into a symbolic representation, most often into words (language). Information gathered in the present is integrated into our existing memories, links are automatically made between what we have known and what we just learned, and ties are established between how we feel now and other memories with similar emotions. A specific memory becomes the combination of the new information and the material that was already stored in memory. Retrieving a memory may involve accessing this combination of information or by accessing an emotional state. We are likely then to recall related memories.

Memories involving trauma appear to operate very differently. The "speechless terror" so often experienced in trauma interferes with the mind's ability to symbolically code this information in language. The brain then records the physical sensory experiences (somatic memory or body memories), or the experiences of touch, smell, sound, taste, and sight. Images, like a mental photograph or a video, may be stored. These memory traces appear not to fade or be distorted by incoming information (as occurs with our normal memory processes) as there are no symbolically mediated associations. The traumatized person does not have stored memories that can connect with these experiences.

Traumatic memories are recalled in processes that differ from normal memory recall. The images of the trauma may impinge upon one's awareness, without warning. Because the memory involves sensations and images (rather than words or thoughts), the experience may seem as if one is reliving the trauma. It may be very difficult to determine what happened back then and what is occurring now. These "flashbacks" can be very frightening and may cause some-one to feel out of control.

During a flashback, traumatized people may actually feel and act as if the trauma is occurring again. They may try to get away, defend themselves, or be very still as they reex-perience the trauma.

Some experience dissociative processes, which are au-tomatic mental inhibitions that can serve to distance one's experience from potentially threatening realizations, ob-servations, feelings, sensations, emotions, memories, or fears. Dissociation alters the experience of the self, that awareness and sense of who I am. The typical sense of self and psychological functioning of the self as a whole, uni-fied person is disrupted. This may take many forms. *Dis-sociative Amnesia* results in the inability to recall impor-tant personal information associated with a traumatic event, such as a flood survivor who cannot recall how he or she escaped from a submerged car. *Dissociative Fugue* is characterized by inability to recall one's identity and the establishment of a new identity following a sudden, unex-pected move or travel. A person may disappear from the community and be found only months or years later after he or she has established a new identity.

Multiple Personality Disorder, or *Dissociative Identity Disorder*, is also believed to be a protective strategy against trauma. The establishment of unique and separate identi-ties with their own memories, feelings, and abilities is thought to be an attempt to isolate the part of the self that encountered the trauma. In such cases, each personality state is experienced differently and separately from the oth-ers, as if the same body housed several people.

Another common dissociative defense for traumatized persons is *Depersonalization Disorder*. While a trauma-tized person retains an orientation to present reality, they experience a sense of detachment or estrangement from themselves. It is as if they are living in a dream, watching themselves in a movie, or are outside themselves looking in. Often, they feel as if they are not in control of their own actions or speech, that life is happening to them and they are passive observers, blocked from themselves. People who witness a loved one being murdered may detach themselves from the scene, not only what they observe but also what they sense, think, and feel. Should this become a frequent way of coping with reality, they may describe their experience "as if I were living."

"I Just Want to Avoid It All"

The long-term aftereffects of trauma are often characterized by attempts, both conscious and unintentional, to avoid thoughts, feelings, or reminders of the trauma. Many experience emotional numbing, or a sense of restricted emotional reactions. The highs are not so great, the emotional lows seem less intense, and all of life may seem as if in fog, as if seen from afar. The emotional reactions appear to have little impact on daily life.

Thoughts, feelings, conversations, movies or TV shows, books, or any other reminder of the trauma may be avoided. Social relationships are often curtailed. A new distance develops between one's self and old friends; new friends are not sought or are kept at a distance. Old activities no longer seem attractive—participation is reduced or discontinued.

Traumatized people may also try to avoid the future, believing, perhaps, that they will not live long, that their future is short. They tend to have difficulty planning, focusing on the here and now.

In the midst of these tendencies and attempts to avoid all memories of the trauma, intrusive thoughts and feelings often break into awareness. Without warning and seemingly out of context, a memory, thought, image, or statement will spring into consciousness, disrupting everything else. These thoughts may not be logical and, for some, involve false accusations of guilt. For others, these thoughts are mental reruns of the traumatic event. Such flashbacks can seem very real, as if the trauma were happening now. Not only are the thoughts the same as then, the senses (sights, smell, touch, taste, and hearing) may all be experienced as if the trauma were occurring in the present. It seems too real, as if the trauma is repeated again and again. Wanting to get away from the terror, many traumatized people sense they are forever trapped.

Vulnerability to Further Trauma

Once people have experienced trauma, they often greatly fear further catastrophes. As one survivor of a major flood put it, "I'll never look at water the same." Innocence has been lost, a sense of being protected and safe is now gone.

The effects of trauma are cumulative. As our capacities to cope are finite, we tend to become more vulnerable to experience trauma following traumatic events. An event that would have been distressing may become traumatic if the individual is depleted or already overwhelmed. The timing of subsequent traumas also impacts the experience and capacity to cope. Typically, time is needed following a trauma to adjust. When a person has several traumatic events occur over a short period of time his or her coping resources will be even more depleted and the sense of disorganization and pain will be magnified.

Trauma changes one's worldview. Following such events, trust and hope are often lost or greatly impaired. Memory and physical functioning are altered. Faith and values are challenged. The overwhelming effects of trauma tax all coping strategies. There are ways, however, for a victim to become a survivor.

9

From Victim to Survivor

"We are hard pressed on every side, but not crushed;
perplexed, but not in despair; persecuted, but not abandoned; struck down, but not destroyed. We always carry
around in our body the death of Jesus, so that the life
of Jesus may also be revealed in our body. For we who
are alive are always being given over to death for Jesus'
sake, so that his life may be revealed in our mortal
body."

—2 Corinthians 4:8–11

*V*ictim: "one harmed or killed by another."

Survivor: "To remain alive or in existence. . . . To live or
persist through."

There are times that our losses seem more than we can
bear. Trauma forces us on a journey we never wanted
and exposes us to the realities of living in a sinful world.
We cannot undo what has happened. But what can we
do?

Hazards on the Journey

Traumatic experiences harm us. In addition to the obvious consequences (physical losses and pain), trauma is harmful in additional ways.

The Shattering of Assumptions

Confronted with a horrible, painful loss, we may feel inadequate to make sense out of what has happened. Little may seem real or make sense. Former beliefs and feelings of safety, trust, and the attitude "it can't happen to me" are gone. Also lost may be a sense of fairness, the belief that "if I do the right thing I'll be okay." New realizations of being helpless and powerless replace former beliefs of being in control and self-directed. Self-esteem is threatened by the powerlessness, thoughts of self-blame, and feelings of shame. Even one's place among other people may no longer seem the same. What is real? Where do I belong?

Such losses also activate our dependency needs. Feeling helpless and vulnerable, many are required (possibly for the first time) to accept help from others. At such times we may feel weak, embarrassed, or childlike. Rather than showing dependency on God and other people, some turn their dependencies toward alcohol or other substances or may even become dependent on the sense of control they get from their own anger.

Secondary Wounding

As if the loss or trauma were not enough, the mourner or traumatized person is subjected to further losses (secondary wounding), which is when the reactions of others only add injury on top of injury. Others may not understand the grief process, the need of the mourner to ask questions or express emotions. The loss or trauma was very difficult to survive, yet for some, the aftereffects are as painful and damaging.

Jeff, recently married, regained consciousness in an unfamiliar hospital, confused as to what happened. Only later did he learn that his wife did not survive the accident. He looked forward to returning home, anxious to be around friends and family. The next two years were much harder than he could have anticipated. He was shocked that friends suggest he date again only a few weeks following the funeral. As one put it, "you need to get on with your life." Three months after her death it started to sink in with him—she isn't coming back. Yet others around him did not want to talk about this any longer and seemed surprised he did. Some suggested he had not grieved appropriately.

Most difficult was the response he received from his in-laws. Without directly saying so, he sensed that they held him responsible for their daughter's death. He had been driving, although he had no memory of the accident. When he shared how hard it was for him, they responded "at least you get to go on."

Jeff had lost his wife, the person whom he desired to share his life and dreams with. What he discovered is that he also lost his confidence in relationships, in the belief that others could know, understand, and accept him. He had never felt so alone.

Secondary wounding takes many forms. Following the loss or trauma, others often distance themselves from the mourner or traumatized person. They may be ignorant of what to do and, feeling their own discomfort, do nothing. Or, they may experience distress at the realization of the loss or trauma that may activate their own sense of vulnerability. This distance may be accomplished by disbelief, denial, discounting, or blaming the victim. People with the best intentions may contribute to secondary wounding; they think what they are doing is helpful.

Another form of secondary wounding is manifested in punishment or humiliation of the victim, judging him or her for what has happened. The rape victim who is ridiculed for "being available," the grieving mother who lost her child and is accused of "trying to get attention," or the traumatized person whose symptoms are minimized as "he was always a little crazy" are all examples of secondary wounding.

Victim Thinking

Trauma does its greatest damage when we lose contact with who we are and begin to identify ourselves with the trauma. Old definitions of reality are no longer adequate; other people seem like perpetrators, new events are potential traumas, relationships are too vulnerable and risky because of the potential for loss.

Victim thinking colors every experience. Below are listed some of the beliefs a person who is locked into victim thinking may display.

- Others have power; I am weak.
- I can't change my situation.
- I have to stay angry or someone will take advantage of me.
- I am helpless, powerless.
- I am unlovable.
- I can't trust anyone.
- Life should be fair.
- There is nothing I can do.
- I have to have others' approval or understanding.
- I can't afford to make a mistake.
- Other people treat me poorly on purpose.
- I need someone to take care of me.
- I'll be okay if only you . . .

- I can't handle it.
- I'm entitled after what I've been through.
- I'm never going to be able to recover from what has happened.
- I'll never be happy again.
- God loves others but not me.

Such victim thinking can lead to a victim identity, that is, a self-definition centered on being a victim. We may have no awareness of this yet be greatly influenced. Such beliefs may be evident to those who know us before we see them ourselves.

Victimization vs. Victim Identity

Losing oneself to a victim identity distorts one's very nature, value, and relationship with God. Victim thinking leads to passivity, helplessness, and other distortions.

Being aware of these unrealistic beliefs and expectations can be a starting point in the adjustment process. Listed below are a sample of some unrealistic, dysfunctional beliefs that may increase one's vulnerability to victim thinking.

- I should never feel hurt, loss, or pain.
- Life should be fair.
- I should be able to protect my children from pain or loss.
- It is wrong to be angry.
- God will give me everything I want.
- God will bless me because I've earned it.
- Others should please me.
- I should please others and they should appreciate this.
- Others should know what I want or need.
- Relationships should be easy, or at least not this hard.

- God has abandoned me if I'm in pain or don't get what I want.
- I should be able to find a rapid solution to my problems.
- Life shouldn't be this hard.

The presence of these and similar beliefs increases the likelihood of victim thinking and identity. Disguised in many forms, these beliefs are common in our culture and may give a false sense of power, self-righteousness, and order.

Overcoming Victimization: Becoming a Survivor

What does it mean to be a victim? The experience of trauma truly does victimize; there are real "victims." They have experienced something horrible and, in that context, we call them victims of that dreadful event. However, this is not who they *are*—it is not their core identity. The title "victim" simply identifies a role that was imposed upon them, and a historical experience they had.

A New Identity

Trauma can leave us detached from ourselves, unsure of who we are. How can we define ourselves after what has happened? Rather than allowing an event (the loss or trauma) define who I am, I can learn to choose to be a person living in the present who has, in the past, experienced a loss or trauma. The loss or trauma can be interpreted through a filter based on truths greater than a single experience. From this new vantage point I can connect with something bigger than me, facilitating a reconnection within myself. My body may never function again as it had; I may, for instance, always have an exaggerated startle response. However, I may also have a new, deeper, more realistic view of reality.

My identity must be defined by something greater than the loss or trauma. Who I am now includes who I was before as well as who I am now. I can integrate my past (including the trauma), my present, and thoughts of the future.

Christ offers us a true identity, one in which we learn to view ourselves as God sees us. Truths offered to us in the Scriptures, such as that God will never abandon us (Deut. 31:8) or that we can be equipped and strengthened in Christ (Phil. 4:13) need to be embraced. Just as the dysfunctional thoughts need to be challenged and purged (see Appendixes 5 and 6), reality thoughts can be rehearsed, reviewed, and brought into our awareness. Christ, who suffered trauma so that he could bring us back to himself (redemption), offers us a relationship in which we can know that we are loved, clean, forgiven, and have an eternal future with God in peace, safety, justice, and righteousness.

Traumatic experiences change us forever. For some, past trauma is analogous to an inoculation. Prior traumatic experiences may strengthen us to live with the realities found in a sinful world. Our identity in Christ can transform our dependencies away from unrealistic beliefs and others, and toward eternal truths and the living relationship we have with our heavenly Father.

Resiliency

Many who have experienced trauma cope quite well. Psychologists call this ability *resiliency*. A husband-wife research team, the Wolins, were challenged by the findings that the majority of people who are raised in alcoholic homes function well and do not become alcoholic. They have studied the successful coping strategies of these individuals, and observed that the losses and traumas did leave their marks but that these scars could be used as strengths. Seven clusters of resiliencies, listed below, were defined as coping strategies, responses to the challenges presented by their losses and traumas.

- *Insight*: the habit of asking tough questions and giving honest answers.
- *Independence*: drawing boundaries between yourself and troubled others; keeping emotional and physical distance while satisfying the demands of your conscience.
- *Relationships*: intimate and fulfilling ties to other people that balance a mature regard for your own needs with empathy; the capacity to give to someone else.
- *Initiative*: taking charge of problems; exerting control; a taste for stretching and testing yourself in demanding tasks.
- *Creativity*: imposing order, beauty, and purpose on the chaos of your troubling experiences and painful feelings.
- *Humor*: finding the comic in the tragic.
- *Morality*: an informed conscience that extends your wish for a good personal life to all of humankind.

These resiliencies or learned characteristics, develop out of the pain and threat of the losses and trauma and help with coping and living well. Trauma changes us, harm does occur in the victimization, but we are not ruined.

Holding onto what is true, to what is ultimately real, can be the foundation of our identity. This perspective recognizes the realities of pain, suffering, injustices, and loss. Yet our lives are more than this. Paul observed this when he wrote the following:

> As it is written: "For your sake we face death all day long; we are considered as sheep to be slaughtered." No, in all these things we are more than conquerors through him who

loved us. For I am convinced that neither death nor life, neither angels nor demons, neither the present nor the future,
nor any powers, neither height nor depth, nor anything else
in all creation, will be able to separate us from the love of
God that is in Christ Jesus our Lord (Rom. 8:36–39).

We can cope, knowing that we are not alone, that our
thoughts and feelings matter to God, and that nothing can
ultimately destroy us.

Coping with Trauma

People who have experienced traumatic loss often need
very specific and concrete ways to cope with their own reactions and anxieties stemming from the trauma. The goal
of this chapter is to identify these specific strategies.

With our identity in Christ, we can learn to cope with the
changes that trauma has forced upon us. The goals of coping with trauma are similar to those for resolving grief. Following a traumatic experience, we need to adjust our understandings of the world, of other people, of ourselves,
and of God. We need to find a way to establish a sense of
personal safety and meaning in life. In addition, the physical effects and intrusive experiences must be addressed.

Our bodies are designed to adjust to even the most horrible and terrifying situations. We can learn to live well after
trauma yet the trauma will always affect us. We will not be
able to live as if the trauma never occurred, although many
will try. Some of our attempts at coping with trauma will
be automatic; other coping strategies need to be learned.

Automatic Coping

Our automatic coping strategies, or defense mechanisms,
serve to protect us from an awareness of overwhelming
feelings, thoughts, and sensations. Our defense mechanisms protect us from focusing on potential or real danger,

freeing us to live our lives. For example, few of us pay attention to the ordinary things we do that are dangerous (statistically speaking), such as driving a car or taking a bath. We would be anxious and unable to function in our daily world if we focused on such potential dangers. These strategies are most often very helpful but can be harmful if used to excess or at times when no objective danger exists. People can be overwhelmed and very anxious if their defense mechanisms are either too great or too weak.

People display many automatic coping strategies when they have encountered trauma. Below is a partial list of these defense mechanisms.

- humor
- suppression (of anything undesirable)
- dissociative defenses (see the previous chapter)
- depersonalization (experiencing a sense of detachment from self)
- intellectualization (using thinking to avoid feeling)
- repression (unconscious removal of awareness of unacceptable memories, thoughts, or feelings)
- denial (lack of awareness of stimuli or events in reality)
- splitting (separating reality into distinct "good" and "bad" elements)
- acting out

Learning to identify the defense mechanisms that may be in operation can greatly assist trauma survivors in coping with their present lives and even appreciate how wonderfully we are designed. We are created in such a manner that we can cope and, with God's love and grace, we can thrive.

The intrusive thoughts and feelings regarding the trauma that can be so disturbing often serve an important function. In a dynamic process a balance exists between the controls (or defense mechanisms) that determine how much emotional pain is experienced and what memories are allowed into awareness. If the controls are inadequate, memories and painful emotions flood and disable the person. In contrast, overcontrol diminishes the person's overall emotional availability and interferes with or inhibits the adjustment process. The optimal process is termed *oscillation,* or the moving back and forth between exposure to the realities of the trauma (including intrusive memories and flashbacks with all the accompanying pain) and freedom from these thoughts and feelings (including emotional numbing and avoidance). At such times the individual can focus on present living.

Coping Choices

Not all of our coping options are outside our awareness. We can learn much about how we have been effected, how our bodies, minds, and emotions respond, and about our relationship with God. We are not ultimately helpless; we have many choices.

Learning about the effects of trauma on the body, mind, and soul can help us be realistic in the ways we cope. The physical experiences we have, such as a racing heart rate, may not mean what they did prior to the traumatic experience. For many, their emotional measuring stick has been modified. Events that used to cause an emotional reaction with an intensity of a "3" (on a 10-point scale, with 10 being "most intense"), may, for a traumatized person, produce a reaction with an intensity of "7." Learning about the effects of trauma can help us redefine for ourselves what is happening in our bodies and around us.

We can learn to self-monitor our experience, to take measurements of our feelings, muscle tension, or any other aspect of our experience. Learning to self-monitor has at least four advantages. First, paying attention to what we feel or how our body is reacting can help us realize that we are not helpless. The choices we make influence how we feel, think, and how our body responds. Second, self-monitoring helps us become more acquainted with our "posttrauma" response style. Our reactions to sounds, events, people, or feelings is different following the trauma. Self-monitoring introduces us to our new self, it helps us become aware of who we are and how we react. Third, self-monitoring is the first step in a change process. And fourth, our acceptance of ourselves and our own reactions can grow as we become more aware. Research has consistently shown that as we monitor and record what we think, feel, or do we tend to make changes that are healthy and desirable. (Further instructions and models for self-monitoring are provided in Appendix 2.)

As we become more aware of our own physical reactions, we can learn to reduce excessive anxiety, muscle tension, fatigue, anger, or general physical arousal. There are many strategies for reducing this physical hyperactivity, some of which are identified in Appendix 3.

You can also learn to ground yourself; that is, to distinguish what is happening in the present from what occurred in the past in order to moderate the disorienting consequences of dissociation or flashbacks. Examples of such strategies are provided in Appendix 4.

As we become more familiar with our new reactions and increase our perception of control in our life, the effects of the trauma lessen. It is not reasonable to expect that things will be "as if nothing happened." This kind of healing is not like the repair to a car in which you replace a part and the car runs as good as new. Rather, it involves changing, growing, learning more about ourselves, others, and God. Healing involves a continual coming to terms with reality, both the reality of our experience and of our faith.

10

A Word of Hope

"We do not want you to be ignorant about those who fall asleep, or to grieve like the rest of men, who have no hope."
—1 Thessalonians 4:13

This book is not about an easy subject. The losses that produce grief, be they the ordinary losses of life or the jarring experiences of trauma, are, indeed, the hardest things we will ever face in life. We have examined how we experience grief, what causes it, what we can expect in its development, and some of the spiritual issues that it raises.

The last word, however, ought to be a word of hope. Let us remember, then, some of the truths that will help us get through the journey of grief.

Grief is a journey with a conclusion.

God has designed us with the internal ability to adjust to life's most jarring losses. That adjustment will not take place in a matter of days or even weeks if the loss was severe. Months and years are more realistic. This is not to say that if a loved one dies that you will not be able to cope for a very long time, but rather, that you will be affected and that you will continue to adjust your inner and outer life for a long time. We instinctually look for ways to cope from the outset, and, with God's grace, we will find ways to make it through long days and sometimes longer nights.

But with the passage of time the journey will be completed. Sometimes we take just baby steps, at other times we make longer gains. The completion of the journey does not mean that our memories will be erased. Even when we approach the end of the journey that does not mean that in future years we will not have a stab of pain when we remember the time of separation when the loss occurred. But we will have learned how to change our lives to a new, adapted, mode of living.

You don't need to go on the journey alone.

Your loss is your loss, and in that sense, you are alone. No one can truly come alongside you and say that they know exactly what you are going through (although we should not be surprised when other people try to say that). However, there are people who have come through the same *kind* of thing that you have. If you lost a child, or a spouse, or a parent, or a job, or a marriage, there are others who have come through the same journey. Most important, there are people who have come through the other side. Seek them out. Tell them your story. Don't expect that any one person will have all the wisdom, insight, and compassion you are craving in your loss—but do take whatever support you can from the assurances of others who have been enabled to go on with life even after being knocked to the ground.

No one can take from you the living memories, the reality, of the good things that you experienced with whomever you lost.

We would experience less pain if we never had anything or anyone to lose, but that would only be our own poverty. If you are coming through the experience of grief, it is probably because there was something or someone good in your life whose absence you now are starkly aware of. That you were able to appreciate what you had is to your credit, and you carry with you into the future the same capabilities to love and to value.

Though you cannot build new memories, no one can take from you the warm and positive memories of the one you lost. You were probably changed as a person because of those experiences, and that you carry with you into the future. If you were made a better or fuller person because of a close relationship, then you have been permanently changed for the better, and that ennobles the life of the person who is now gone.

God has offered himself to you in your grief.

The fact of suffering does not mean that God is not real or not available. We have been told that we live in a fallen and broken world that is full of the frustrations of conflict, disease, and death—that we can see with our own two eyes. Our grief would be no easier to bear if we decided that God must not be around—indeed, at times of loss we need him more than ever. God has promised that he would not leave us alone, that the lives of creatures like us who experience pain and suffering will ultimately be restored and healed if we hold onto him, and that it is possible to be reunited with those whose final destination is an eternal relationship with him. When Jesus left his disciples he could see the pain in their eyes. He told them that they would grieve for a while, but that their grief would turn to joy.

Indeed, in the life of Jesus we see God himself experiencing all of the basic kinds of loss we go through. He was betrayed by friends, rejected by those he came to help. He wept at the tomb of a friend and shook with fearful anxiety on the night before his own arrest and death. He saw people trashing their lives, and making a mockery of everything that really matters to God.

But he also saw more. He saw the brilliance of the resurrection after the darkness of the tomb. He saw us, capable of standing before God clothed in righteousness. He knows us to be smoldering wicks and bent reeds. But instead of snuffing us out or breaking us, he gives us grace to go on.

When we face tragic loss we may not feel very strong in faith. But we must remember that faith, at its core, is the weak and troubled person throwing himself or herself on the mercy of God. And if we do so, we will find ourselves borne up.

> Do you not know? Have you not heard? The LORD is the everlasting God, the Creator of the ends of the earth. He will not grow tired or weary, and his understanding no one can fathom. He gives strength to the weary and increases the power of the weak. Even youths grow tired and weary, and young men stumble and fall; but those who hope in the LORD will renew their strength. They will soar on wings like eagles; they will run and not grow weary, they will walk and not be faint (Isa. 40: 28–31).

Grief
and Specific Populations

While the phases of grief are universal, the experience of mourning is shaped by many factors.

Grief and the Death of a Child

Nothing seems as unjust as the death of a child. The loss of one who seems to have so much potential, so many life experiences ahead seems so unfair. While less common than in generations past, over 50,000 children die each year in the United States. Our cultural expectations of a long, healthy life may leave us unprepared to cope.

Families are forever changed following the death of a child. Naturally, parents don't want to forget their child. This healthy desire can inhibit the grief process as some conclude that if they adjust, if they live well now, they will forget and it will seem like the child is no longer important.

Family members have a great need to talk about the deceased child, to recount stories and share their emotions and thus be assured that they will not forget the child, that others who are close to the family will not either.

One's own death is often contemplated, even to the point of wishing for or considering suicide as a way to be with the child. In one study, 50 percent of mothers of deceased children no longer looked for happiness but were waiting for their own death.

A search for meaning, a cause, or a rationale for the death is common. Approximately 70 percent of parents who have had a child die seek spiritual solutions and increase their commitments in their religious communities. Many seek to be reunited with their children in heaven yet also are looking for meaning in a painful world. A significant and lasting change in values occurs in which traditional Western values of achievement and success are diminished and the values of family, relationships, and spirituality are strengthened.

While most family members will make a positive adjustment to the loss, a phenomena termed shadow grief often remains, a lingering grief that is always in the background and behind everything else, which may persist throughout life. Anniversary dates, such as the date of the death, Christmas or other family holidays, when the child's class graduated, or when the child's friends marry may elicit further grief responses. This normal reaction requires further adjustments, further letting go so that the mourner may invest in the present world.

Grief and the Death of an Unborn Child

Deaths of children not yet born also elicit grief. A miscarriage, even in the first few weeks, is very likely to elicit mourning. Frequently, the woman will initially blame herself or, to a lesser degree, her husband. Grieving this loss is complicated if others did not know about the pregnancy. No one will have had the same attachment to the developing child as the mother. She will likely experience a fantasy about what the child would have been like, how it would have looked and acted. Her husband is likely to focus on action or diversion, attempting to get on with life. In addition, if any attention is received by the couple during their mourning, it is likely to be directed toward the wife, further alienating the man from his grief.

This pattern frequently elicits conflict between the couple. Sometimes husbands or wives expect their spouses to grieve in the same manner they do and suspect that the other is denying his or her pain. To lessen this conflict they need to realize that they have different experiences and different relationships with the child.

Similar to the grief response following a miscarriage, mourning may occur following an abortion. Such grief is complicated by the willful decision to have an abortion and often by a time delay between the loss and the recognition of the loss.

Grief and Men

Traditional masculine values, such as being strong and taking charge interfere with the work of grief. Letting go and accepting the loss seem incongruent with masculine traits.

Men tend to grieve alone, in silence. Little is said. Men tend to return to work or other activities soon after the loss and busy themselves with their activities. During the initial stages of grief, men are often in the role of making decisions, caring for others, making sure everything is taken care of. Grieving becomes the role of the women and children. Following the funeral or the initial adjustment to the loss, men often find the focus is now less of grief and more of "moving on." Having barely begun their mourning, they bury themselves in work or increase their use of alcohol or other substances. A widower is likely to visit the grave alone and express his pain through crying, words, or other expressions. Other people may have no awareness of his graveside visits or tears.

Feeling out of control, men are more likely to take legal or physical action in response to a significant loss. For some, grief is replaced by anger, aggression, and even violence. Risk-taking behaviors may increase as a demonstration of perceived personal power and life. The use of alcohol, drugs, or other substances may increase.

While the pattern of solitary, silent mourning is common, it is important to note that this pattern may be out of perceived necessity rather than choice. Men often receive messages from others that cue them to keep their pain private. A question such as "how are the kids holding up?" directs the focus of the man's grief toward others. Men frequently want to express their thoughts and feelings and, when given a chance in a safe situation, will do so. A recent study of widowers found that 97 percent of the men expressed relief when given a chance to express themselves.

How can men be given a chance to be heard? Men often need some time to determine if it really is safe to proceed and an acknowledgment of the appropriateness of expression. Direct questions, such as "How are you doing?" "Are you sleeping okay?" or statements such as "I've been concerned about you" may help establish the initial connection. Furthermore, men tend to benefit from multiple contacts. A follow-up call, a breakfast, a basketball game followed by some quiet time can facilitate a continuation of the expression and sharing necessary for grief resolution.

Grief and Children

Children who experience great loss, such as the death of a parent or sibling, have the same grief work, the same need to adjust to the loss, as adults. However, children must make these adjustments within the parameters and limitations of their developing abilities. Furthermore, as new thinking, emoting, and relating abilities develop, they may have to grieve the loss again in the context of these new abilities.

A child's concept of death develops from no awareness of time or permanency during infancy to the adult's understandings. Preschool children think of death as a nonpermanent sleep, a reversible event. School age children (ages 5–9) often think of death as coming from the outside, from a monster, an angel who takes away life. Even at this age, death is thought to be something that can be reversed, outwitted, or avoided. In the child's thinking, "If I do the right things, death will not happen." When death occurs, a child is likely to blame himself or herself, assuming an exaggerated sense of responsibility.

As the child matures and begins to develop abstraction abilities, death is understood in biological terms and, while seemingly distant and avoidable, appears to be irreversible. It is common for teenagers to alternate between fears of death and risk-taking behaviors with a sense of being invincible.

A child's mourning is greatly shaped by the developmental stage he or she is in. Fears are common—e.g., that the surviving parent will die, or fears of going to sleep. Often children experience a loss in safety and security and revert back to earlier coping strategies. School age children may return to sucking their thumb or carrying a blanket following a parent's death. Children long to know they will still be protected, cared for, and that they will not be alone.

Anger toward the one who died, toward the loss, or toward the survivors caught in their own grief is also a common reaction. They may experience abandonment and conclude they are unimportant, weak, or powerless. In the immature thinking of children, they may conclude their parent died because they were not loved by the parent or were bad. Many children have interpreted the death of a loved one as a punishment. Others have thought their anger "wished" them dead or somehow that they themselves made the death occur.

A child's understanding, limited by their stage of development, is often confused. Not only do they have difficulty understanding the implications of the death, they are confronted with unexpected changes in all areas of life. How does God fit into this? Even young children take some comfort in thinking "Mommy is in heaven" yet may be angry or feel left out that they can't be there also. Children long to be reconnected with the deceased. Their need to be connected in a relationship must be a primary focus of their caregivers.

Adults need to be sensitive to the child's stage of development and need to allow or facilitate the child's expression of their thoughts and feelings. One young woman shared that as a child she was told "God loved your mommy so much he took her home to heaven to be with him." It is not surprising that this young woman had difficulty seeing God as good or loving. How could a loving God be so selfish as to rob a child who needs her mother so he can enjoy her company?

Children, like adults, need to proceed through the tasks of grief. How they proceed is greatly influenced by their level of development and how the adults in their world are mourning.

Grief and Cultural/Racial Differences

Mourning is a learned process, acquired in childhood through observing how family members and others in the community react to death and other losses. Different cultures have developed unique strategies for processing grief. Some cultures, such as northeastern Brazilian mothers, who experience a very high infant mortality rate, express very little grief upon death. Other groups express a great outpouring of emotion, such as Egyptian mothers, who may display wailing and crying for days or weeks followed by years of muted depression, the suffering a link to the deceased. Still others manifest their grief through somatization (physical symptoms that mimic illness, such as the chest pain of "a broken heart"), aggression, or pscyhologization. Western cultures have tended to define grief in terms of the symptoms and problems of the experience rather than appreciating the value and purpose of grief.

We need to be sensitive to our learned patterns and accept both what we have learned about mourning as well as our unique needs to grieve. In addition, it is inappropriate to expect that all people will grieve in the same ways. Grief can be effectively processed in many different ways.

Coping with Trauma: Strategies for Self-Monitoring

Learning how to be aware of what we think, feel, and how we act can be helpful in many ways. The aftereffects of trauma may include both emotion numbing and the experience of intense and unpredictable feelings. Learning to monitor your emotional reactions can help ease the pain, provide understanding of what is happening, and assist you in making choices in daily living. The following two strategies can help you to gain a sense of self-control and hope.

The Emotional Awareness Scale (EAS)

You can learn to be aware of how you are feeling by rating the intensity of any emotional reaction at a specific time. Using a 10-point scale, you can assign a numerical rating to your present experience. This will help you identify what you are feeling now as well as help you track your emotions over time. In this way, you can become aware of the times you feel good (which are often not remembered if you do not write them down) or determine if there are any patterns in your feelings. For example, do you feel worse in the mornings or at times you stay home?

Time:
Place:
Activity:

0 ← ————————————————————————→ 10
(low)   (high)

These ratings may be made in a journal or on a small card carried in a pocket. Any emotion may be monitored, and often it is helpful to track several emotions simultaneously, such as happiness, fear, and anger. In addition, some find it helpful to make an overall, summary rating of the day and keep track of their emotional state over many months.

Thought, Feeling, and Action Scale (TFAS)

Increasing your awareness of the relationship between your thoughts, feelings, and your behaviors can help you identify the control you do have in your life, clarify your choices, and help you be responsible for yourself. The following exercise can help you focus on these relationships.

Event	Interpretation (Thought)	Emotional Reaction	Action/ Behavior

After listing the event, you can identify how you interpreted it and what you thought about it. In addition, you can notice and record how you felt at the time. Sometimes your thoughts will be easier to identify, while at other times you will be more aware of your feelings, which will influence how you choose what action to take. This form of self-monitoring may be used to look back at something that has already happened and fill in all four categories, or to use it as an aid to deciding what action to take.

Strategies for Reducing Physical Tension

The excessive physical tension that can come with fear, anger, or fatigue can be a real problem, and can be relieved through some simple activities, a few of which are listed here.

Physical Exercise

Regular physical exercise that results in a sustained increased heart rate for no less than 20 minutes three to four times per week can provide a general state of decreased tension, but also may help decrease uncomfortable feelings and a sense of helplessness. Such exercise need not be extremely strenuous. Walking, swimming, or bicycling can provide these benefits.

Healthy Breathing

We can learn to release unneeded tension by developing healthy breathing habits. Bringing breathing under voluntary control can also combat thoughts of helplessness or being out of control.

A simple, deliberate sigh can release tension—a technique that can be used anywhere. Begin by allowing yourself to just let go of the air in your lungs, letting out a sound of relief as you exhale through your mouth. Then, allow yourself to breath in naturally—do not force yourself to inhale. It is likely you will notice a brief moment between exhaling and inhaling, a brief time of peace. You can repeat this process as often as desired.

One can also use deep breaths to release tension. Begin by inhaling through your nose and imagine you are filling the bottom third of our lungs, then the second third, and finally filling them completely. In doing so, your chest and abdomen will expand and shoulders rise. After a brief moment, you can slowly release the air. You will notice your shoulders will relax, followed by the muscles in your chest and then abdomen. You can then repeat this process a couple of times, often leading to a sense of feeling momentarily refreshed and more relaxed.

Focusing on What Is Good and Pure

There are many strategies for changing your thoughts and awareness. You can reduce your physical tension and increase relaxation by telling yourself what is true (some options are offered in Appendix 6). Or you can calm yourself by imagining yourself in a safe and comfortable place. Many find comfort in focusing on the 23rd Psalm, allowing themselves to feel content in the Lord, sense lying down in green pastures, and being reassured that "they will dwell in the house of the LORD forever."

Appendix 4

Strategies for Staying Present-Focused

Trauma sometimes causes great disorientation that can be a very unsafe condition. The following activities can help you turn your attention to your *present* circumstances (your immediate surroundings and physical sensations) as a way of living in reality. These strategies can be helpful at times of great distress and confusion or dissociation.

Focus on Immediate Surroundings

- Identify a sound, something you are presently hearing, and determine the source of the sound.
- Identify something you see, focus on it, and describe to yourself the details (size, color, texture, etc.).
- Identify sensations from your other senses (smell, touch, or taste) and focus on the details and characteristics of those sensations.
- Write out truth statements (see Appendix 5).
- Review, either silently or out loud, your identifying information, such as your name, age, address, phone number,

marital status, and names of your spouse and children (if applicable) as well as today's date and your present location.
- Read something that is a favorite, something soothing or calming.

Interact with Other People

- Ask for a "reality check." Ask a trusted person if he or she is having the same experience or interpretation as you.
- Choose to make eye contact with a trusted person.
- Ask for a hand or a hug. Focus on the warmth, texture, and strength of the contact.

Focus on Specific Physical Sensations

- Push your feet against the floor, noticing that the floor is solid, resists your efforts, and will safely hold you.
- Work Silly Putty, Play-Doh, or clay in your hands. Focus on the texture and resistance of the substance while noticing your muscles and the sensations you experience while squeezing, pulling, and twisting it.
- Purposefully focus on your breathing. Count each time you inhale or exhale. Feel your chest and abdomen rise and fall as you inhale and exhale. You may place your hand on your abdomen and feel it move, expanding as you inhale and contracting as you exhale.
- Rub your hands, legs, or feet. Focus your attention on the sensations.
- Change the position of your body. Sit differently or stand if sitting.
- Stretch your muscles, yawn, sigh, or otherwise release physical tension.

Again, the purpose of these activities is to get past the mental confusion or disorientation that traumatized people sometimes experience.

Appendix 5

Strategies for Changing Troublesome Thoughts

Intrusive or recurrent thoughts of past trauma or of possible future harm may plague the traumatized person. The Apostle Paul, a man acquainted with trauma and grief, wrote that we do not need to be controlled by such thoughts.

> Do not be anxious about anything, but in everything, by prayer and petition, with thanksgiving, present your requests to God. And the peace of God, which transcends all understanding, will guard your hearts and your minds in Christ Jesus. Finally, brothers, whatever is true, whatever is noble, whatever is right, whatever is pure, whatever is lovely, whatever is admirable—if anything is excellent or praiseworthy—think about such things (Philippians 4:6–8).

You can learn to train your mind to attend to what is true and pure. In addition to prayer, the following strategies, when practiced, can help you develop a sense of healthy control over your thoughts.

Thought Stopping

Troublesome, disruptive thoughts can occur following a trauma and interfere with present coping. The following strategy can be used to develop increased focus of attention on desired truths.

Thought stopping involves the following five steps:

1. Identify the unwanted thought. Once identified, list the negative characteristics of the thought, such as how the thought is hurtful or unrealistic.
2. Identify the context of the unwanted thought. The TFAS can be helpful.
3. Thought Interruption. As the unwanted thought begins to occur, startle yourself to stop the unwanted thought. You may say (shout) "STOP," make a fist, snap a rubber band on your wrist, or any other activity that startles and disrupts your chain of thoughts. The startle activity may be either overt or covert.
4. Thought Substitution. Replace the unwanted thought with a truth statement, such as those listed in Appendix 5.
5. Follow-up. Repeat steps 2–4 as often as necessary. This skill will take much practice to develop.

It is important that the replacement thoughts be about truth. This technique will not work well if the substituted thoughts are unrealistic. Often, it is very helpful to talk with a trusted person about this process, identifying both the unwanted thoughts and truth statements.

Changing Distorted Thoughts

Unrealistic, distorted thoughts about yourself, others, God, or your situation can be changed using the following four-step strategy:

1. Identify what you are feeling.
2. Describe the situation. Define what has happened in detail.
3. Identify what you are thinking about the situation or event. Determine if your thinking is distorted or unrealistic. Often, it is very helpful to talk with a trusted person at this point.
4. Refute the distorted thinking by identifying what is unrealistic and replacing it with truth statements.

Appendix 6

Truth Statements

Do not conform any longer to the pattern of this world, but be transformed by the renewing of your mind. Then you will be able to test and approve what God's will is—his good, pleasing and perfect will (Rom. 12:2).

The following statements can be read, written, repeated, and focused on at times of confusion, alienation, and distress. It may be helpful to write out the statements that are most meaningful to you and carry the statements with you. The statements can be reviewed many times per day, providing a reminder of what is real.

- I won't always feel this way.
- Joy will return someday.
- Life is a mix of joy and sorrow.
- Emotional pain hurts, but that doesn't mean it is harmful.
- "In this world you will have trouble" (John 16:33).
- God is greater and stronger than any other person or force.
- God is stable—life is not.
- Life is not fair.

- Evil is real.
- God knows me and loves me.
- Jesus knows how it feels to suffer—he also suffered.
- It's okay to be angry when something is wrong.
- It's okay to cry—Jesus did.
- It's okay to have needs—our lives are in vessels of clay (2 Cor. 4:7).
- It's okay to be scared—God is with me.
- God is with me even when I don't feel it.
- God loves me no matter what I feel.
- God will give me strength when I am weak.
- It's okay to say no.
- The truth is always my friend, even when it is painful.
- I can make it through my pain—God will be with me.
- It's okay to speak the truth in love.